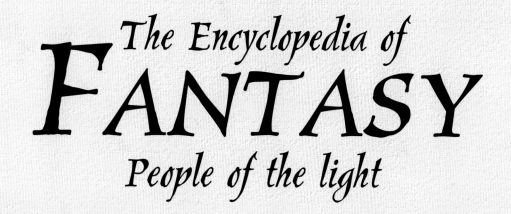

The Encyclopedia of
FANTASY
People of the light

À tous les magiciens du verbe et toutes les fileuses de paroles.

Dedicated to word magicians and spinners of tales.

The Five Mile Press Pty Ltd
950 Stud Road, Rowville
Victoria 3178 Australia
Website: www.fivemile.com.au
Email: publishing@fivemile.com.au

Cover design Aimee Forde
Graphic design Élodie Saracco
Original illustrations Sandrine Gestin
Chapter head illustrations Alain-Marc Friez
Translated into English by Lorraine David
Formatting in English translation Diana Gibbs

National Library Cataloguing-in-Publication Data
Brasey, Édouard.
Encyclopedia of fantasy : people of the light.

1st ed.
Bibliography.
Includes index.
ISBN 1 74178 243 0.

1. Fantasy fiction, Australian. I. Title. (Series :
Encyclopedia of fantasy ; 1).

A823.4

Printed in China

The Encyclopedia of
FANTASY
People of the light

Édouard Brasey

The Five Mile Press

Writer, storyteller and scenario-writer, Édouard Brasey has explored the world of the imaginary and invisible for more than fifteen years. A former journalist and holder of many diplomas in a variety of fields, his stories most often centre around fantastical legends, quests and dreams, and the presence of other beings among us and other realities above. He has published many works in French, and his English works include *Faeries and Demons, and Other Magical Creatures* and *Dragons, Little People, Witches, Fairies, Trolls and Elves*. When he is not traversing elfin kingdoms and dreamlike realms through his writing, he is travelling to other countries and researching their histories, writing scripts and giving conferences and shows inspired by mythologies and fairy tales. He has also published several novels. Check out Édouard's website at www.edouardbrasey.com

contents

Preface

Elves, fairies, imps, angels, mermaids and sirens, genies, centaurs, dwarves or gnomes. Was the earth once inhabited by all these beings, or did we simply invent them? The age in which we live already has the answer: things can only be real if they can be proved scientifically. So we have sylphs or korrigans, comfortably classified as imaginary creatures, alongside the yeti or the Loch Ness monster. Yet nothing which is imaginary is pure invention. The ogres of our fairy tales, devourers of warm flesh, developed out of the horrible memories of the Hungarians – formerly known as the Huns – and Attila who feasted on raw meat, and whose speed on horseback is echoed in the story of the seven-league boots. Closer to our day, the orcs described by J.R.R. Tolkien in *The Lord of the Rings* were born out of the Nordic sagas, which told of strange peoples from the Orkneys, north of Scotland, who were in fact Picts. The African pygmies do not refer to themselves by that name: they were called "pygmies" by the explorers, in reference to Greek mythology.

Does this mean then that marvels or the imaginary do not exist? Quite the opposite, in fact. The imaginary world is just like a painting. The landscape exists, but the artist transforms it into a work of art. Thus, the ogre is no longer simply a Hun, but a reflection of our fears: the ogre and the bogeyman may also represent adults who harm children. The bloodthirsty Hun has become an archetypal creature, pushing his extreme savagery beyond human boundaries. Already inhuman, he is transformed into a monster and a creature of the marvellous. Most of the creatures described in this volume have undergone a similar transformation from the real to the imaginary. Fairies, the most emblematic creatures in the world of marvels, probably descended from Celtic druidesses and forest goddesses, which the Romans of the same period called *fata* (from *fatum* meaning "fate"). In the Middle Ages, fairies were the representation of an inaccessible feminine ideal: mysterious, refined and beautiful ladies for whom one died of love. In seventeenth century tales, they gained a magic wand and appeared as "godmothers", before finally becoming minute creatures endowed with wings. What links are there between the Celtic druidess and *Peter Pan's* Tinkerbell? Perhaps none at all, except that fairies too are an archetypal model to which the human soul aspires. They express our fascination with beauty, fragility and grace, and also, as with elves, our dream to stay close to nature and understand her secrets. We are no longer dealing with monsters, but superior, superhuman beings who are generally kind and beautiful. They possess a divinity, just like angels, muses and genies.

So did tiny tinkling fairies like our friend Tinkerbell in *Peter Pan* really ever exist on Earth? We would like to believe so. In any case, we can believe that in ancient times there existed peoples who were different – either because of their habitat, their appearance, and sometimes their cruelty, as was the case with the Huns – who have become legendary, and have been absorbed into our culture. This encyclopedia of the extraordinary aims to gather systematically, for each of these creatures, all the various sources which have fashioned their identity: history, legends, mythologies, folklore, literature and cinema. Anything which has helped to shape our present-day view of them. Enthusiasts of fantasy, the fantastic or the marvellous, whether they be "hooked on" role play, computer games, comic strips, literature or cinema, will find amongst these pages plenty to feed their passion, as they discover the fascinating origins and evolution of all these creatures. In these times of cultural globalisation, the extraordinary history gathered here by Édouard Brasey reminds us of the no less extraordinary wealth of diverse cultures that have contributed to the world of imaginary beings – a world which is anything but imagined!

JEAN-LOUIS FETJAINE

Once upon a time there were marvels

in anything at all, but at the same time we question what lies hidden behind this emptiness, and our search has an air of foreboding.

WHAT IS THE MARVELLOUS?

Unlike the fantastic, where supernatural elements become involved in everyday life, the marvellous assumes magic exists and forms the framework of our lives. While the fantastic instills doubt and fear in the minds of readers or spectators, the world of marvels offers dreams and enchantment – even though sometimes the dream may turn to nightmare and the enchantment to a spell. The fantastic creates situations which by definition are impossible, but which occur against all logic, whereas the marvellous, although it has evolved from a purely imaginary universe, nevertheless feels authentic and real; in a word – natural. Historically we associate the marvellous with medieval culture, wherein belief in fairies, elves, imps and mermaids was a part of everyday life. People believed in fairies just as they believed in the devil. It was only with time, the development of rational thought, and a preoccupation with scientific process that former beliefs became legends which were handed down in the form of folktales. But despite the aspirations of the Enlightenment, reason and science cannot provide an answer to everything. Medieval faith was rooted in religion, but heavily influenced by the marvellous. At the same time, this fervour was tinged with doubt and fear, interwoven with agnosticism and traces of the fantastical, tearing holes in the fabric of reality. The ancients believed in fairies, and sometimes they even saw them. Contemporary culture no longer believes

A RETURN TO SPIRITUALITY

If such is the case, now, with the birth of a new century, why produce this *Encyclopedia of Fantasy*? Simply because we are witnessing a return of spirituality which – like religious fervour - seeks out its ancestral roots. "The twenty-first century either will or will not be spiritual," declared Andre Malraux. Renewal of interest in marvels implies a return to the world of childhood and magic, where wishes come

It is on the night of Saint John that the Little People are the most active...

responses which are perfectly adapted to the challenges facing a world which today seems to lack meaning and values. Many present-day movies and books are clearly inspired by the marvellous.

THE PEOPLE WHO INHABIT THE WORLD OF MARVELS

The *raison d'être* of this encyclopedia, which will extend to several volumes should God and those bands of inspirational fairy godmothers remain willing, is to provide detailed, reliable and documented information on the origin and description of entities to be found in this world of marvels: characters, beasts, places, things and creators. We have begun by dividing into two groups the peoples who inhabit this marvellous world: People of the Light, to be found in the present volume, and People of the Dark, who will be the subject of a subsequent volume. Of course, in the world of marvels, the borders between dark and light are not always as clear as reason might wish. This becomes obvious to any reader glancing through the pages which follow; while people of the light include good fairies and kindly elves, we also find there misshapen dwarves, fearsome goblins and cruel mermaids. Rarely are fairy-tale creatures perfectly good or totally wicked; they do not have our human moral ethics, and often their behaviour seems unpredictable. Our research has necessarily been limited to Western culture, although certainly there are Asian, Oriental and other equally rich indigenous versions of our world of marvels, which in themselves would require yet further volumes!

true and dreams become reality. It also aims to add a dash of re-enchantment to the world, by viewing it through eyes filled with wonder. The current infatuation of audiences with quests for adventure, rites and passages of initiation, tales of chivalry, and fairy tale legendary worlds – whether in literature or cinema – has led to a rediscovery of the exploits of King Arthur and the Knights of the Round Table, Tolkien's *Lord of the Rings*, the *Star Wars* saga or the sorcerer's spells taught in that strange school attended by Harry Potter. This confirms that far from being buried away on a dusty old moon, the world of marvels offers

For our purposes, we have explored Greek and Roman, Celtic, Germanic and Nordic mythologies, as well as certain other influences which have come to enrich our European traditional cultures: thus we shall introduce the reader to Oriental djinns, Latin fauns, Nordic gods, Germanic dwarves and Breton imps. Some of the more illustrious works which we pored over in search of source material included Paracelsus's *A Book on Nymphs, Sylphs, Pygmies and Salamanders and on the Other Spirits* published posthumously in 1566; *The Secret Commonwealth* by the Reverend Robert Kirk, parish minister of Aberfoyle in Scotland (1691); and Sir Walter Scott's *History of Demonology and Sorcery* (1832).

We had the great fortune to be able to consult a reference work par excellence, the incunable *Traité de Faërie* by Ismaël Mérindol (1466), the only extant copy of which is held at the Prague National Library. As a result, this and subsequent volumes of *The Encyclopedia of Fantasy* are embellished with illuminations and illustrations equal to the best medieval wizards' books of spells.

But now, let us turn the pages together and take a step back into that wonderful universe – but not without first pronouncing that enchanting phrase with which all fairy tales begin: "Once upon a time …"

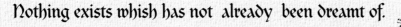

𝔑othing exists whish has not already been dreamt of.

Ismaël Mérindol, *Traité de Faërie*, 1466.

The air people

-1-

The people of the air are the most sophisticated of all the spirits. While they live in the air (although some live in fire), they owe their name mainly to their ethereal grace. These creatures have elements of the divine, and that is why they were often adored and feared by the ancients, and also by angels or elves. Although they are generally kind, like sylphs or genies, they may sometimes be extremely cruel, like the harpies, Erinyes or djinns.

Angels

Appearing in the form of fire creatures, sometimes assuming an androgynous appearance of exceptional beauty and immaculately robed in white, angels are both incorporeal and immaterial, and therefore really are pure spirits. Their name comes from the Greek *angelos*, meaning "messenger". They are divine messengers, between God the creator and his human creatures. It was an angel who appeared in a dream to Joseph to tell him of the miraculous conception of Jesus;[1] again it was an angel who made him flee to Egypt to escape the wrath of Herod;[2]

Illustration:
© Sandrine Gestin

Despite the Byzantines' quarrel on the gender of angels, both male and female angels exist.

yet another bade him leave the land of exile and return to Nazareth.[3] According to the Hebraic Cabal, angels are symbols of divine energy, without being gods themselves. That is why it is blasphemous to adore angels. However, it is permitted to invoke them in prayer, asking for their intercession with the god. In this regard, one must not confuse angelic invocation and demonic evocation. The former is related to prayer or white magic, and the latter to black magic.

1 and 2. Matthew, II, 13.
3. Matthew, II, 9.

ANGELIC HIERARCHIES

Daniel describes the host of angels thus: "A fiery stream issued and came forth from before him: a thousand thousands ministered unto him, and ten thousand times ten thousand gathered in his presence."[4] Psalms says that "the chariots of God are thousands upon thousands of angels: the Lord is amidst them".[5] And Saint John declares: "Then I looked, and I heard around the throne and the living creatures and the elders, the voices of a multitude of angels, numbering myriads of myriads and thousands of thousands."[6] The Cabalist Rabbi Isaac Luriah estimated the number of angels to be sixty myriads. Pseudo-Denys the Areopagite established in the celestial hierarchy an order for angels organised into nine choirs and three triads.

The first triad consists of the first three orders of angels:
– Seraphims (meaning "the burning ones"), fire angels sitting by the throne of God and endowed with six wings: "two to cover their face, two to cover their feet and two to fly";[7]
– Cherubins, who spread the fullness of their wisdom;
– Thrones, who are fixed immovably at the foot of the divine throne. The second triad consists of Dominations of the virtues and powers, full of quiet authority, and freed from all impediments. Lastly, the third triad, further from divinity but closer to man, and thus more accessible, knows the principalities, the archangels and also the angels. The most famous of them is Michael, prince of the celestial armies (this name in Hebrew means "resembling God"); Gabriel

4. Daniel, VII, 10.

5. Psalms 67.

6. Revelation, V, 11.

7. Isaiah, VI, 1-2.

("the force of God"), angel of the Annunciation to Mary; and Raphaël ("God's remedy"), sent to cure Tobias and Sarah, whose prayers had been offered at the same time in the presence of the Lord, before he appeared to Tobias, saying: "I am the angel Raphaël, one of the seven who stand in the presence of the Lord".[8] Certain angels who had rebelled against God had fallen and assumed the form of demons.

GUARDIAN ANGELS

The existence of guardian angels is a dogma of the Christian faith, and there are many references to them in the Bible. The role of guardian angels is similar to that of friendly genies: they accompany all humans from birth to death, or more precisely from conception to the afterlife, guiding us to good thoughts and works, and preserving us from evil.

They are also mentioned in other religions as well as Christianity. In Islam, for example, everyone has not one but two guardian angels: "Muslims believe that people all have two guardian angels each, one to note down the good deeds they do, and the

other the evil. These angels are so good that whenever someone they are watching over does something bad, they let him sleep before recording the action, in the hope that he will repent upon waking".[9] In Persia, each individual has not two but five guardian angels watching over them. "The Persians have five guardian angels for each person, the first placed on his right to record his good deeds, the second on his left to record the bad, the third before him to lead the way, the fourth behind to protect him from demons, and the fifth on his brow to elevate his thoughts towards the Prophet." [10]

Germanic and Scandinavian Gods

Ases, asynes (fem.), vanes

Firstly, "the gods" must not be confused with God. The latter, a monotheistic being who is adored by all religions, is unique. Gods, however, being descended from ancient

pantheons and antique mythologies, must be classified with the people of the air. Of all the mythologies, only the ases dwell in the sky, unlike the Greek and Roman gods or divinities, for example, whose Pantheon or Empyrean is on a mountain peak on Earth.

Ases and asynes are warring gods and goddesses of Germanic and Scandinavian mythology. Their name comes from the "as" rune, meaning "ancestor-god". They are related to the vanes, divinities associated with the functions of fertility, pleasure and love. Their leader is the one-eyed god Odin, called Wotan in the Germanic version from which Richard Wagner drew the inspiration for his opera

Ases, asynes, vanes

8. Book of Tobias, 3, 25.
9 and 10. Collin de Plancy, *Dictionnaire infernal*, 1825–1826.

*Painting (right):
Thor's battle against
the giants, 1872, Marten
Eskil Winge, oil on
canvas, ©
Giraudon/Bridgeman
Art Library*

The Rhinegold. In his celestial realm of Asgard, the fortress of the gods, known as Walhalla in German, he reigns along with his two sons, Thor (whose famous hammer, Mjöllnir, makes thunder whenever he throws it), and Baldur (nicknamed "the Good" because he is considered the best of the ases). Odin is accompanied by the gods Loge (god of Fire and a thief, sower of strife and the very incarnation of evil), Freyr, Njödr, Tyr, Heimdallr, Vidar, Bragi, Vali, Hoenir, Forseti and Ullr.

The goddesses are called Fricka (wife of Odin), Freya (goddess of Love, who watches over the apple of eternal youth, and ensures immortality of the gods), Sigyn (wife of Loge), Gefjon, Gerdr, Idunn, Fulla and Nanna, as well as Syn, Vör, Var, Eir, Lofn, Ljöfn, Hlin, Gna and Snotra.

THE WAR OF THE GIANTS

The kingdom of the ases, known as Asgardr or Walhalla, is situated in the heavens beside the Sun and the Moon, and is linked to the Earth – Midgard, inhabited by Man – by a bridge called Bilfröst, in the form of a rainbow. This celestial palace was built by a giant, with the help of his horse Svaldifari. It was agreed that if the giant could build this palace within a given time, he would win as his reward the vane goddess Freya, as well as the Sun and

the Moon. To avoid paying this exorbitant price, which would have deprived them of the main sources of cosmic light, and of eternity, the gods resorted to trickery. Loge, the master of metamorphosis, transformed himself into a mare on heat, to attract Svaldifari, leaving the giant to complete the task alone. At this the giant broke into such a terrible rage that the gods were fearful, and implored Thor to crush his head with his hammer. From the mating of Svaldifari and the mare Loge was born an eight-hooved charger called Sleipnir, which Odin took as a warhorse. In the Edda, a collection of mythological tales, we read that the ases were at war with the hoar-frost giants whom they massacred. The first one they killed was Ymir, whose body, cut into tiny pieces, served to create the world.

VALKYRIES

In Scandinavian mythology, Valkyries are the war-loving virgin daughters of the ase Odin. Tall and beautiful, with a proud and aristocratic bearing, they have deep blue eyes and thick blonde hair. They wear winged or horned

helmets and metal breast-plates for protection, as they gallop off astride their flying chargers. Whenever a battle breaks out on Earth between rival clans, Odin sends the Valkyries to assist in the combat. Each one chooses the hero whom she feels is the most valiant and deserving, and should he be mortally wounded, bears him off to Walhalla, the celestial home of the gods and resting place of wounded soldiers. They play a similar role to that of guardian angels in the Christian religion.

These chosen soldiers assemble in a vast hall with walls covered with shields, spears and bloodied swords. They have engaged in violent battles, but their injuries are miraculously cured, and they gather joyfully around Odin to celebrate. They eat roast pork washed down with mead or strong beer, poured into horn cups for them by the beautiful, proud Valkyries, who have transformed themselves from war-mongers into maid servants.

Between battles, the Valkyries roam the Earth in the form of

Painting (above): The Ride of the Valkyries, *XIXth century, William T. Maud, oil on canvas,* © *Giraudon/Bridgeman Art Library*

The Valkyries changed themselves into swan-maidens

Doppelgängers, co-walkers, hemzâd, Ka

Siegfried), who removes her armour and wakes her with a kiss. They fall in love, but when Brünnhilde learns that Sigurd really prefers the magician Gudrun, her traitorous lover is assassinated, and she sets herself alight. Richard Wagner also found inspiration in the historical character of Brunehilde the Merovingian; widow of Sigebert (grandson of Clovis and whose name is related to the variants Sigurd/Siegfried), she was the first Queen of France.

THE TWILIGHT OF THE GODS

The Germanic and Scandinavian gods are not immortal, since their end comes with Ragnarök, the Germanic and Scandinavian apocalypse which Wagner popularised under the name "The twilight of the gods". The monstrous wolf Fenrir, chained up by the ases, breaks free and devours the sun and the moon, while Midgardr's serpent emerges and causes a deluge. The giants cross Bilfröst, the rainbow bridge, and invade Walhalla, where they kill the ases, assisted by Fenrir and the serpent. The world of the gods is destroyed, but the sun

reappears above the Earth, where a man and woman, who were miraculously saved, repopulate a world in which henceforth there are no gods.

Doubles

Doppelgängers (Germany), co-walkers (England), hemzâd (Persia), ka (Egypt)

An individual's double is his "other self" who accompanies him throughout his life and even survives his death; but this entity is different from the shadow, the guardian angel or the friendly genie. It is the "astral body" in opposition to the "physical body", known to the Egyptians as ka. When a person dies, the double leaves the body of the deceased and briefly appears in the form of a ghost. Sometimes it may leave the body of the dying and show itself to the person. That is why according to legend "see one's double, then die".

So that a double may more easily fly away when a person dies, and so that it will not remain on Earth as a ghost, it

white swans, closely resembling the swan-maidens of Celtic mythology. Some of them choose to leave Walhalla and live on Earth simply as mortals. Then they are renowned not only for their beauty, but also for their healing powers. Richard Wagner's opera "Die Walküre" is based on a combination of this mythology and the early thirteenth-century *Song of the Nibelungen*. His heroine is the Valkyrie Brünnhilde, who disobeys Odin (Wotan) by granting victory to a soldier who was fated to die. Odin punishes her by casting her into a deep sleep, her body covered with a shield and protected by a wall of fire. She is saved by the hero Sigurd (Wagner's

is customary in Britain and in Germany to open wide the doors and windows of a house where someone has died, and drape the mirrors so that the double has nowhere to hide. Unlike guardian angels, the double may prove troublesome when he appears alone, especially following the death of his "original". Such is the case of the German doppelgänger. In some extreme cases of split personality, the doppelgänger can take control of his "original" and cause him to commit horrible crimes, such as in Stevenson's *The Strange Case of Doctor Jekyll and Mr Hyde*.

Christmas Eve is the sign that the person will die during the coming year.

When a person dies, his shadow goes to hell, but it may stay awhile in the place where the deceased lived and died; it becomes a spectre or ghost. It is said that animals are able to see shadows of the dead, and especially cats, which sometimes bristle without any apparent reason, or fix their eyes on an invisible form.

Whosoever sells his soul to the devil no longer casts a shadow in the sunshine, as was the case for the tragically famous Peter Schlemihl.[11] And so it is with vampires.

SHADOWS

The shadow is distinct from the body and the soul, and represents a state midway between the two, but an integral part of the individual. The shadow is the dark side of a person's double.

We must take great care not to walk on another person's shadow or to throw stones at it, for fear of affecting his health: the magic spell known as 'enclouage' or pricking consists precisely of treading on the shadow of the victim. The projection onto a wall of a person's headless shadow on

Djinns

Genies, djouns, efrits, djinniya (fem.)

According to Arab legends, the djinns are spirits of the air, and the Koran divides them into kind genies who faithfully follow the teachings

of the Prophet, and rebellious demons. Generally invisible, they can sometimes appear in the form of vapours or flames, or else they take on the appearance of hideous giants with feet buried in the Earth and heads lost in the clouds, just like the djinn whom Hasan al-Basri met in a tale of *The Thousand and One Nights*: "It was a demon whose head was as big as an enormous dome, with teeth like a dog's; his gullet resembled a goat-skin gourd, and his nostrils the mouthpiece of trumpets; his ears were like great leather shields, and his mouth the yawning entrance to a cavern; his teeth were like stone pillars, his hands like pitchforks and his feet like yard-arms. His head reached the sky and his feet sprang from

Genies, djouns, efrits

11. Peter Schlemihl,
Chamisso, 1814.

Illustration:
© Sandrine Gestin

*Elven, Tylurithes,
Tyluryth Teg,
elfen, Daoine
Sidhe, siths,
elfen, nis, alfen,
nis, god-drange,
huldras, Tom-
Gubbe, Tanttu,
duende, esprits
follets*

12. *Les Mille et Une Nights*, translation by Bencheikh and Miquel, Folio, Gallimard.

the bowels of the Earth."[12] These spirits inhabit deserts or graveyards, and prefer to move about at night. One can tell they are present by a whistling sound, or puffs of air which are borne on the wind. It is they who create little swirls of sand in the desert, who cause hikers to stumble in the darkness, or who mingle with humans by assuming the appearance of an animal. They are the culprits who spread diseases such as cholera, rheumatism, epilepsy and madness, which is a form of possession by djinns. To ward off evil djinns, it is traditional to invoke a benediction from Allah before meals *(Bismillah)* and to take care to avoid confronting one's own reflection in a looking glass during the night. Djinns fear the light of day, gunshots, music, the joyful, piercing screams of women during weddings, salt, steel, hemp, benjoin and henna; that is why the women have spells drawn in henna on the palms of their hands and the soles of their feet.

There are also female djinns known as djinniya, who closely resemble our European fairies.

Elves

Elven, tylwithes (England), tylwyth teg (Wales), elfin (Scotland), daoine sidhe, siths (Ireland), elfen, nis (Germany), alfin (Scandinavia), niss-god-drange (Denmark and Norway), huldras (Norway), tom-gubbe, tonttu (Sweden), duende (Spain), esprits follets (France)

Essentially spirits of the air, but also of the forests and the hills, both male and female forms are to be found. Elves originated in Scandinavian mythology (alf, plural alfen), as incarnations of the spirits of the dead, but the Anglo-Saxon term (elf, plural elves) associates them with fairies and other members of the Little People in general. The term "elf" thus includes relatively different creatures, which must be classified in a more detailed manner.

FAIRIES, DEMONS OR LORDS?

In the Nordic legends, elves were divided into light elves and dark elves. Light elves, which evolved from the air, appear as sylphs or angels, while the dark elves, having chosen

to inhabit the depths of the earth, live in the company of dwarves, gnomes and demons.

The forest elves are little winged characters of childlike appearance and proportions, often with green-coloured skin. They flit among the treetops, and may be recognised by their evil eyes, which slant upwards to the temples, and by their characteristically pointed ears. They are related to the woodland fairies, being their male descendents. Lastly, the noble elves resemble very tall humans in every way, endowed with a proud beauty and refined bearing, and dressing after the fashion of the medieval lords. They

resemble the forest elves only because of their pointed ears, known as "elfin ears". Tolkien's elves fall into this category.

TUATHA DÉ DANANN

These noble elves are created from the Tuatha dé Danann, or "tribes of the Goddess Dana" – Dana being a goddess-mother from the Celtic Pantheon. This elfin race originated from the mysterious isles of the northern hemisphere (Hyperborealis) who were later to inhabit Emerald Ireland, after having first driven out the *fir bolg* or lightning-men, tribes of blacksmiths. Immortal and eternally youthful, they in turn were displaced by the Milesians, who were to give rise to the Gaelic peoples.
Following the battle of Tailtiu, today known as Teltown, in the County of Meath, an alliance was formed between the Tuatha and the new Masters of Ireland, with each group taking its share of the island: the Milesians occupied the surface, while the elves took the underground parts, building whole cities and subterranean palaces hidden under the green hills and mounds of Erin. The Tuatha were endowed with magical powers, and were often consulted by the men living on the surface above them.

THEIR POLITICAL POWER

Just like the Tuatha dé Danann, the noble society of elves is strictly hierarchical, and based on a monarchical-theocratic model. The supreme sovereign of the Tuatha was named Dagda, meaning "god of good", but he was also known as Ollathair, or "the father of all". He had many sons, each of whom reigned over one of the subterranean counties of Ireland. The most famous of them was Oengus, nicknamed Mac Oc, or "younger son".

DAOINE SIDHE, OR SITHS

Once known through legend and folklore, the Tuatha dé Danann came to be called daoine sidhe, or siths, that is "hill people".
The Reverend Robert Kirk describes them thus: "These fairies or siths have a nature falling somewhere halfway between man and angel, like the ancients considered the daemons; intelligent and curious by nature, they have lithe and fluid bodies somewhat akin to a condensed cloud, and are best seen in twilight. Their bodies are very supple, due to the subtlety of the spirits that move them, so they are able to appear or vanish at will. Some have bodies or forms which are so spongy, so fine, and so lacking in density that they take their nourishment simply by sucking up a thin liquid which penetrates like pure air or oil. Others are nourished by grains and liquors or from the corn which grows on the surface of the Earth, and which these fairies glean, sometimes invisibly or sometimes by scavenging like crows and mice."[13]
It is said that during the night of Samhain, or Halloween, enchanted mounds open up, allowing the underground elves to mingle with humans just for one night.
In Scotland there are also subterranean elves, who are cousins of the Irish siths. But they also live in other natural elements, and may be divided into the following groups:

13. Robert Kirk, *The Secret Commonwealth*, 1691, edited by S. Sanderson, D.S. Brewer, 1976.

Forest elves are the size of children. They love to play with beautiful fairy maidens.

Painting (right):
Fairies and spirits in the
woods, *Georges Picard,*
© Giraudon/Bridgeman
Art Library

23

dun-elfen (dune elves), *berg-elfen* (hill elves), *munt-elfen* (mountain elves), *wudu-elfen* (forest elves) and *woeter-elfen* (water elves). In Wales they are called *tylwyth teg* signifying "benevolent family".

THEIR HOMES

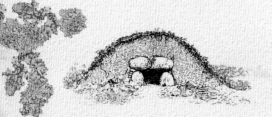

According to Giraldus Cambrensis, the twelfth-century Gallic author, elves lived in a dark land where there was neither sun nor moon, nor stars: "These creatures were exceedingly short, but very well proportioned, with pale skin and luxuriant locks which fell to their shoulders like that of women. They had horses and dogs in proportion to their own size."

The Tuatha dé Danann lived in splendid underground palaces buried under the megalithic mountains and hills of Ireland. The finest of these palaces is called *Brug na Boyne*, and it is filled with treasures and marvels, even the more modest of which would make the most sumptuous human riches pale into insignificance.

THEIR MUSIC

Elves are admirable musicians. The Tuatha dé Danann of Ireland are well known for their skills in the arts, especially in poetry and music. King Dagda was an accomplished musician who was able to coax melodies from his harp which created in turn laughter, tears, nostalgia or slumber amongst his audience. One of his sons, Bodhb Derg, whose subterranean palace was situated in the south of Ireland, kept at his court some very knowledgeable bards, including the famous Cainchinn and his son Cascorach. These unequalled musicians played a sort of Celtic harp, called a tympanum or dulcimer, which they wore slung across their chest when moving from place to place. They played a style of music with such strange and bewitching sounds that it was said Saint Patrick himself, the Patron Saint of Ireland, declared that the elves' music really was most beautiful. Despite being imbued with magical qualities, the saint declared that "no other music is closer to celestial harmony".[14] The best musicians in Ireland, whether fiddlers or bagpipers, are accustomed to drawing their inspiration from some enchanted hillock upon which they sleep, ear glued to the ground the better to surprise the marvellous melodies which seep up from the underground court of the elves. But musicians thus initiated always end up giving in to the irresistible nostalgia which permeates this music. They die overcome by langour and soon leave this world to return to the kingdom of the elves.

In the same way, Norwegain huldras, like the siths, live inside tumuli or in hills; their sublime music, called *huldraslaat*, filters out of their hideaways, and mountain-dwellers can capture it should they put their ear to the ground. Yet once cornered, the elves take revenge by transforming their sweet melodies into a cacophony of lamentation and

The famous Ismaël Mérindol, fifteenth-century scholar to whom we owe the magnificent *Traité de Faërie*, which is still considered a standard work of reference today, often had occasion to hear the marvellous music of the elves during his youth. He describes it thus: "Often times, before beard grew on my chin, amongst the leaves rustling in the wind I heard a multitude of choruses resounding with such a harmony of sounds that no Earthly voice, whether that of maid or boy, could hope to equal their enchanting splendour. Alas, such concerts, which drew tears from my eyes and caused my heart to rejoice, one day became inaudible, by which time hair had appeared on my cheeks and elsewhere, and the clock pendulum which hung heavy between my thighs had grown appreciably longer. For by a strange turn of human fate, only virgin boys and maidens are able to enjoy the ethereal music of the elves."

14. *Silva Gadelica*, edited by S. H. O'Grady, 1892.

sobbing, thus plunging overly curious listeners into a deep state of melancholy which can be fatal.

Generally speaking, whatever their country of origin, elves love to play, dance and cavort endlessly, both within their enchanted palaces and at night in the forest. But at the sound of the cock's crow, all that remains of their passing is the faint impression of footprints in the grass.

ELF-SHOT AND ELF DISEASES

Elf-shot consists of a spear head or a flintstone which the hunting elf throws with extraordinary skill in the direction of his prey. Elf-shot is widely used to decimate herds. Reverend Kirk recounts his experience in Scotland: "Their arms are made partly from strong earthly materials without any steel, but mostly they use stone resembling soft yellow spa flint which they shape into barbed arrowheads and throw with force like darts. These arms (seemingly manu-factured with superhuman instruments and craftsmanship) have the force of thunder and mortally wound the vital organs without breaking the skin; I

have observed this type of wound in animals and touched them with my own hands."[15] Besides their deadly elf-shot, elves are guilty of causing many illnesses which affect beast and man alike. These include such disorders as madness and epilepsy (called *ylfig* or "elfique" in Old English); urticaria (*elveblest* in Norwegian, *alfarbrunni* in Icelandic); colic (*alvskot* in Danish); acne rosacea (*Elffeuer* or "elf's fire" in German); and lumbago (in German *Alpschuss*).[16] The Laeceboc and the Lacnunga, two tenth-century English pharmacopoeia described dis-orders such as "water elf sickness" and "elves' disease", which are treated with an unguent consisting of holy water, absinthe, fennel, incense, lichin and the lower part of an "enchanter's shadow".

These same compilations warn against cattle diseases caused by the elves: "If a horse or other beast has been wounded by an elf's dart, take some sorrel seed and Scottish wax and have a man sing twelve masses over it. Sprinkle holy water over the horse, and whatever the wound, always keep some of these plants handy."[17]

To protect oneself from the

poisonous breath of elves, a fifteenth-century German charm suggests the following:

Hook-nosed Elf,
Don't breathe in my face!
Elf, I forbid you to smoke,
To crawl or to breathe!
You demon sons of elves,
Don't touch me with your claws![18]

15. Robert Kirk, *The Secret Commonwealth*, 1691, edited by S. Sanderson, D.S. Brewer, 1976.
16, 17 and 18. Cited by Claude Lecouteux, *Les Nains et les Elfes au Moyen Âge*, Imago, 1988.

Familiar Genies

Familiar demons, familiars, genies, daemons, guardian spirits

Plato claims that familiar genies are invisible, but Apuleius believes the opposite is true. Plutarch declares that sneezing is the usual sign of genies. Socrates had a demon whose advice he sought in all circumstances. One day the demon warned Socrates against taking a certain path. The philosopher heeded that advice whereas his companions continued on their way; further along they encountered a herd of swine and arrived covered with mud.[19]

FAMILIAR DEMONS

Many famous people had a familiar genie to serve them, among them Popes Benedict IX (elected in 1033) and Alexander VI (elected in 1492), whose familiar demon later went on to serve Caesar Borgia. A monk from the Abbey of Citeaux also had a familiar to wait upon him and help him tidy his room, until the day the Abbot discovered the genie's presence and banished the monk from the monastery. The demonologist Jean Bodin (1530–1596) made mention of a man whose familiar spirit would box him over the left ear whenever he conducted himself poorly, or to alert him to someone with evil intent. Others were Cecco d'Ascoli (Italian physician and astrologer, 1269–1327), Cornelius Agrippa (German alchemist and philosopher, 1486–1535), Paracelsus (physician and alchemist, 1493–1541) and Jerome Cardan (Italian mathematician, 1501–1576). Paracelsus kept his genie in the pommel of his sword, which never left his side. He used it as his valet and secretary. Jerome Cardan, who discovered the solution to quadratic equations, had in his service a familiar spirit inherited from his father, Facio Cardan. Collin de Plancy wrote: "Like Socrates, he claimed to have a familiar demon which he considered to be half-human and half-divine, and which

communicated with him through dreams. He then admitted that he owed all his talents, his vast learning and his greatest ideas to his helpful demon."[20] The count of Saint-Germain, a celebrated eighteenth-century alchemist, also had a familiar who gave him prudent advice in a loud rumbling voice. King Henry III (1551–1589), fourth child of Catherine de Medici, had received as a

Familiar demons, familiars, friendly genies, demons, tutelary deities guardian spirits

19. William Jones, *Credulities Past and Present*, London, Chatto & Windus, 1880.
20. Collin de Plancy, *Dictionnaire infernal*, 1825–1826.

present from some magicians "a familiar called Terragon. It is thought that he slept with Terragon, and that he 'married' him to the Countess of Foix. But she could not bear his lusty company and presence. Henry III was accused, most imprudently, of one day summoning a prostitute for his familiar, and causing the poor wench to almost die of fright."[21] The Emperor Napoleon Bonaparte also had a friendly genie called "the little red fellow", who advised him and predicted the future. He announced forthcoming victories at Austerlitz, Friedland, Iena and Wagram, and in broad brushstrokes described Napoleon's accession to the empire, his fall from power and finally his exile.[22] It is said that President George Washington also had a friendly genie. In an article published in *Scribner's Magazine* in January 1888, Robert Louis Stevenson (1850–1894), author of

Treasure Island and *The Strange Case of Doctor Jekyll and Mr Hyde*, relates how much he is indebted to his friendly genies, which he calls his "brownies". He explains that it is they "who do one-half my work for me while I am fast asleep, and in all human likelihood, do the rest as well, when I am wide awake and fondly suppose I do it for myself. The whole of my published fiction should be the single-handed product of some Brownie, some Familiar, some unseen collaborator, whom I keep locked in a back garret, while I get all the praise and he but a share (which I cannot prevent him getting) of the pudding."
For Stevenson, these creatures "are near connections of the dreamer's, beyond doubt; they share in his financial worries and have an eye to the bank book; they share plainly in his training; they have plainly learned like him to build the scheme of a considerate story and to arrange emotion in progressive order; only I think they have more talent; and one thing is beyond doubt, they can tell him a story piece by piece, like a serial, and keep

him all the while in ignorance of where they aim. Who are they, then? and who is the dreamer? Well, as regards the dreamer, I can answer that, for he is no less a person than myself. And for the little people, what shall I say they are but just my Brownies, God bless them!"
And let us not forget the talking cricket, Pinocchio's friendly genie.[23]

21. Jules Garinet, *La Sorcellerie en France; histoire de la magie jusqu'au XIXe siècle*, Paris, 1818, reprinted, François Beauval, 1970.
22. Cited by Éloïse Mozzani, *Magie et superstitions de la fin de l'Ancien Régime à la Restauration*, Robert Laffont, 1988.
23. Carlo Collodi, *Pinocchio*.

Salamanders

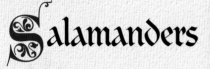

Like sylphs, which are formed from the purest atoms of air, salamanders come from the most subtle parts of the fire in which they live. They are ethereal creatures who have no connection with those fabulous but real lizards which share the same name and are also said to live in fire.

According to the Cabalists, "the salamanders live in fiery regions and serve wise men, but they do not seek out their company; their daughters and their wives are rarely seen. Of all the elementary beings, salamanders live the longest".[24]

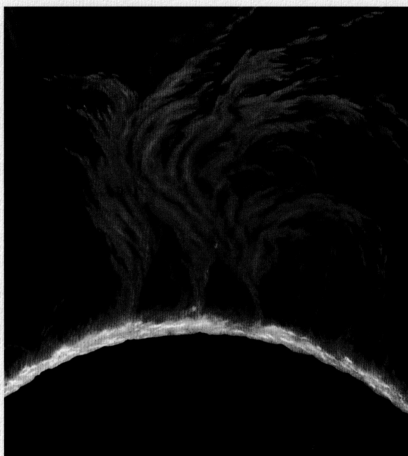

Salamandes are fire creatures, dear to alchemists

HOW TO EVOKE SALAMANDERS

Based on reports by the Count of Gabalis, Collin de Plancy indicates the simplest way to call them forth: "To gain power over the salamanders and have them at your command, you must attract the Sun's fire using concave mirrors in a glass ball; a solar powder is thus formed which purifies itself by excluding all the other elements, and when this is swallowed it draws out the fire within us, and we become igneous matter, so to speak. The inhabitants of the fiery globe will then be inferior to us, and will show us all the affection they show to their kind, and all the respect they owe to their creator."[25]

Symbolising the purifying fire of alchemy, salamanders traditionally fall into four categories corresponding to the different degrees of combustion they have undergone: salamanders may be red, orange, yellow or purple. In the *Comical History of the States and Empires of the Worlds of the Moon and Sun,* Hector Savinien Cyrano de Bergerac describes a salamander bathing in flames, while two fiery beasts symbolising the elements of sulphur and mercury attack one another.

In his memoirs the Italian writer and artist Benvenuto Cellini (1500–1571) tells how as a child he saw a salamander materialise out of the fire at

24. Abbé Montfaucon de Villars, *Le Comte de Gabalis*, Paris, 1670.
25. Collin de Plancy, *Dictionnaire infernal*, 1825–1826.

Illustration (right):
© Sandrine Gestin

home. When his father gave him a resounding slap, the young Benvenuto began to sob, shocked at the injustice of this. Then his father said to him: "My boxing your ears is to remind you always of this exceptional moment when you actually saw a salamander in all its glory."

SENSUAL SALAMANDERS

Female salamanders are extremely beautiful. The Count of Gabalis affirmed that "Salamanders' wives are beautiful, and even more beautiful than all others, for they are from a purer element."[26]
In 1893, the French novelist Anatole France (1844–1924) published a strange work entitled *At the Sign of the Queen Pedauque*, in which he parodies these

alchemistic questions most comically. Supposedly set in the early eighteenth century, the action stems directly from the themes treated in the *Comte of Gabalis*, published by the Abbot Montfaucon of Villars in 1670.
The hero and narrator of the story is Jacques Menetrier, or Tournebroche, so-named because it was his task to turn the rotisserie spit for his father, under the shop sign "Queen Pedauque"; he interrupted his work only to hear the lessons taught by the Abbot Coignard and his novice, Brother Angel.
One day he received a visit from a strange "philosopher", Monsieur d'Astarac, who rushed towards the ashes in the fireplace of the premises.
"A salamander! A salamander!" he shouted.
"And taking heed of no-one, he leant over the fireplace and began to rummage through the cinders, poking at them with the tip of his cane to the great discomfort of Brother Angel who, having swallowed soot and ash with his soup, almost coughed his heart out. But the man in black continued to stir the fire, crying out: 'A salamander! I see a salamander!'

while the agitated flames cast a shadow in the shape of a great bird of prey on the ceiling."[27]
Neither Monsieur d'Astarac nor Anatole France seemed to differentiate between salamanders and sylphs; these ethereal creatures live in similar elements, and above all they enjoy happy relations with humans, even forming romantic ties with them. "These clouds, these soft vapours, these puffs of air, this gleaming light, these waves of blue, these drifting isles of purple and gold which float above our heads are the domain of two adorable peoples. They are called sylphs and salamanders. They are infinitely handsome and lovable. It is possible and acceptable for us to form relationships with them, the delights of which surpass our imagination. Salamanders are so exquisite that in comparison, the finest lady at court or in the town is nothing more than a repugnant hag. They willingly seek out and give themselves to philosophers."[28]

26. Collin de Plancy,
Dictionnaire infernal,
1825–1826.
27 and 28. Anatole
France, *La Rôtisserie de
La Reine Pédauque*,
Paris, 1893.

Ghouls

Stryges or striges, strix, streghas (Corsica)

These genies of the air resemble Greek winged mermaids, or birds with the breasts and faces of women. They are similar to harpies

both in their appearance and their cruelty. Charlemagne condemned the crimes of the ghouls, who are related to larvae, ghosts, phantoms, witches and werewolves. Collin de Plancy writes: "In this passage we read that the Saxons believed that there were witches and spectres (in this case vampires) who devoured or sucked from live people; that they were torched; and that to protect themselves from the voracious habits of these ghouls or vampires, they must needs eat their flesh. Something similar happened with regard to vampirism in the eighteenth century. Another proof that the ghouls of the ancients were sometimes vampires is that in Russia and in some parts of modern Greece, where vampirism wrought its havoc, vampires are still known by the name striges."[29]

In one of his fantastic tales, Marcel Schwob describes these disturbing creatures: "While keeping vigil over the dead, one can hear the ghouls: they sing tunes which beguile you and force you to obey them against your will. Their voices are plaintive, soft and fluting as a bird, tender as the whimpering call of a small child; none can resist them."[30]

HARPIES

Found in Greek mythology, harpies too are winged monsters with the body of a bird and the head of a woman, but in addition they have sharp eagles' claws and give off the most vile stench. Their name means "ravishers", for they seize upon the souls of the dead, suddenly, in order to torment them and drive them to hell.

29. Collin de Plancy, *Dictionnaire infernal*, 1825–1826.
30. Marcel Schwob, "Les Stryges", *Coeur double*, 1891.

There are three of them: Aello ("storm swift"); Celaeno ("the dark"), also known as Podarge ("fleet-foot"); and Ocypete ("the swift wing"), all of whom appear as storms. Only the Wind, son of Boreas, can chase them away. They symbolise the depraved passions, obsessive torments and endless remorse.

ERINYES

The Erinyes, sisters of the harpies, have the same appearance and equally cruel behaviour, but their intervention always corresponds to a punishment dictated by a sentence handed down by the gods.

31. Collin de Plancy, *Dictionnaire infernal*, 1825–1826.

Sylphs and sylphides

Symbols of beauty, refinement and spiritual aspirations, the sylphs owe their name to the Latin word sylphus, meaning "genie". Spirits of the air, for they contain the very purest of its atoms, they fall midway between the angels and the elves. According to Collin de Plancy, the sylphs are erudite beings, "obligingly officious towards the wise, but enemies of the foolish and ignorant" and taking as companions and daughters the sylphides, they are veritable "masculine beauties, as the Amazons are depicted."[31]

Diaphanous-looking creatures, they resemble tall, wonderfully handsome youths. Learned, refined, docile and kindly towards humans, they inspire artists and those versed in spirituality. It is said that to pass the time they sculpt the clouds into familiar shapes. The character of Ariel in Shakespeare's *The Tempest* is a sylph. "I am a child of the air, a sylph, even less than a dream," wrote Victor Hugo.

SEDUCTIVE SYLPHIDES

Sylphs and above all sylphides, often take on a human appearance so as to get closer to them and to win their affection.

The Cabalist doctors of the sixteenth century claimed that, like most spirits, they were born without an immortal soul, but could obtain one if they married a human. But the earthly spouse then had to promise never more to have any amorous dealings with simple mortal maids, so as not to offend his ethereal lover.

Nor could these graceful sylphides support coarseness or poor manners. One Bavarian lord had wed a sylphide who had given him several children. But, alas, his supernatural wife had to leave, owing to the fact that he was lacking in taste, cursed like a trooper and smelled of tobacco.[32] Collin de Plancy tells the story thus: "A young lord from Bavaria was inconsolable following the death of his wife. A sylphide took on the appearance of the deceased and presented herself before the desperate young man, saying that God had resurrected her to console his extreme grief. They lived

together for several years, but the young lord was not man enough to be able to retain the good sylphide; one day she vanished, leaving behind nothing more than her petticoats, and him mourning the fact that he had not heeded her wise counsel."[33]

EXTRATERRESTRIALS IN THE MIDDLE AGES

In medieval times, sylphs were said to get about in airships, and were responsible for carrying off human beings, similar to modern-day extraterrestrial kidnappings. This occurred particularly around the time of the Carolingians, as was

reported by the Abbot Montfaucon of Villars: "During the reign of King Pepin the Short, the famous Cabalist Zedechias got the idea of convincing the world that the elements were inhabited by peoples of a nature different from our own. He hit on the solution of advising the sylphs to show themselves in the air to one and all; this they did magnificently. These admirable creatures could be seen in the skies in human form, here lined up in battle formation, marching in orderly rows, or bearing arms, or camped under sumptuous pavilions; and there, on their marvellously constructed airships, drifting in fleets borne along by passing zephyrs.

"What happened then? At first people thought that they were sorcerers who had taken possession of the skies to whip up storms, and drop hail on the harvest. Wise men, theologians and legal men were soon in agreement with the people. Even emperors believed it; and this ridiculous belief was so spread about that the wise Charlemagne, and after him Louis the Debonnair, imposed heavy penalties on all these so-called tyrants of the air. This may be found in chapter one of the Capitulations of both these emperors.

Illustration (left):
© Sandrine Gestin

32. A. de Chesnel, *Dictionnaire des superstitions, erreurs, préjugés et traditions populaires où sont exposées les croyances superstitieuses des temps anciens and modernes*, tome XX of *L'Encyclopédie théologique*, 1856.

33. Collin de Plancy, *Dictionnaire infernal*, 1825–1826.

Illustration (right):
© Sandrine Gestin

During the Middle Ages sylphs and sylphides mated with humans, and gave birth to famous heroes

34. Abbé Montfaucon
de Villars, *Le Comte de
Gabalis*, Paris, 1670.

"Seeing the people, the pedants, and even heads bearing crowns were so much against them, the sylphs resolved to dispel the tarnished reputation of their innocent fleet by spiriting away men from every quarter, in order to show them their beautiful women, their republic and their parliament, then sending them back to Earth in various parts of the world.

"It so happened that one day, in Lyons, three men and a woman were seen to disembark from one of these aerial vessels. The whole town gathered around, crying out that they were magicians, and that Grimoald, Duke of Benevent, and enemy of Charlemagne, had sent them to spoil the crops of the French. These four innocents had such a hard time trying to convince them that they were indeed their fellow countrymen, and that they had been recently spirited away by some miraculous men, who had revealed unheard-of marvels to them, begging them to spread the news. But these stubborn people would hear nothing of it: they were about to cast them into the fire, when Agobard, Archbishop of Lyons, came running at the disturbance. He proved to the people that they were wrong, that men cannot come down out of the skies, and that they were mistaken with regard to these four strangers. He pleaded their case so well that the people were convinced, and let the sylphs' ambassadors go free.

"Nevertheless, since they had narrowly escaped with their lives, they were now free to tell of all they had seen. Nor was this a fruitless task, since you may remember that the century in which Charlemagne flourished was rich in heroic figures. The ladies of the day believed the woman who had visited the sylphs, and by the grace of God many sylphs were immortalised. A number of sylphides also became immortal due to the tale that the three men told of their beauty. All this obliged the people of those times to apply themselves to philosophy, and from thence came all these tales of fairies that one finds in the romantic legends of the time of Charlemagne and thereafter. All these so-called fairies were nothing more than sylphides and nymphs."[34]

The forest people

-2-

The forest people were born in the untamed primeval forests which formerly covered the continents with thick woodland vegetation so dense that no human would have dared venture therein without taking precautions. The reason that travellers lost in the woods often never return is that, to their misfortune, they run the risk of crossing paths with the divinities of nature who dwell there. Some of them are gentle, like the fairies, others mischievous like the goblins, and yet others such as Amazons, will-o'-the-wisps or satyrs are quite hostile.

mazons

In antiquity, Amazons were savage women who lived in the obscurity of forests, forming warfaring communities which were greatly feared by other tribes. Their name signifies "mamma" breast, preceded by the privative prefix "a-": amazon thus means "deprived of one breast", for these females had no hesitation in cutting off their right breast to avoid hindrance when using their bow. They mated with males in neighbouring communities and after giving birth, they returned the male infants to their fathers, keeping only the girls. In addition to their martial skills, the Amazons practised magic, and were capable of paralysing men simply by thought power.

The Hittites, the Mitannians and the Acheans banded together in an effort to exterminate these fierce warriors, who wore as a talisman belts given them by Mars or Ares, the god of War. The Amazon Menippe presented Hercules with her belt to endow him with her strength.

In his work *Bibliotheca historia*, the Greek author Diodorus of Sicily explained that the Amazons travelled widely across the Earth and made war on many peoples, including the Atlantes. "Myrina, Queen of the Amazons, assembled a female army of thirty thousand infantry and twenty thousand skilled equestrians in the cavalry. As defence they wore the skins of the enormous reptiles which are found in Libya."

These Amazon troops travelled to the land of the Hesperides, inhabited by

Illustration: Men fighting Amazons mounted on horseback, *French school, XIXth century, colour lithography after an antique Greek vase,* © *Giraudon/Bridgeman Art Library*

Banshees, Bean
Sidhe, the
"fairy of the
hills", Bean
Nigne, the
"little washer
of the ford",
Caoineag, the
"weeping
woman"

the Gorgones, a nation of giants with petrifying glares. Following this battle, Diodorus continues, "Myrina ordered the bodies of her dead companions to be burnt on three pyres, and she formed three large tombs from mounded earth which are still today called the 'Amazons' tombs'."

Illustration:
© Sandrine Gestin

Banshees

Banshees, bean sidhe, "the fairy of the hills" (Ireland), bean nigne, "la laveuse du gué", caoineag, "the wailing one" (Scotland)

In Scotland and in Ireland, the banshee is a fairy or a ghost attached to certain very ancient clans, who appears uttering horrible screams to announce the imminent death of the lord or one of the members of the family to which it is attached.

THE WAIL OF THE BANSHEE

For those who know it, the wail of the banshee is so terrifying that it freezes blood in the veins and turns the hair white prematurely. It sounds all at once like the howl of a wolf, the call of a wild goose, the sobs of an abandoned child and the cries of a woman in labour. What is more, it is so powerful that it can wake the deepest sleeper and be heard above the sound of the most violent wind.

In Ireland, the banshee frequently appears in the form of a long-haired woman dressed in a green frock and a grey mantle. Her eyes are blood-red from weeping. Walter Scott explains that Irish fiction "assigns to certain families of ancient descent and distinguished rank the privilege of a banshee, as she is called, or household fairy, whose office it is to appear, seemingly mourning, while she ann-ounces the approaching death of someone of the destined race … If I am rightly informed, the distinction of a banshee is only ever allowed to families of the pure Milesian stock, and is never ascribed to any descendant of the proudest Norman or boldest Saxon who followed the banner of Earl Strongbow, much less to adventurers of later date who have obtained settlements in the Green Isle."[35]

Lady Wilde, mother of Oscar Wilde, added musicians and poets to

35. Walter Scott, *Histoire de la démonologie et de la sorcellerie*, translation by M. Defauconpret, Furne Éditeur, Paris, 1832.

the banshees' protégés: "Only certain families of historic lineage, or persons gifted with music and song, are attended by this spirit."[36]

Clearly, Lady Wilde classifies banshees as ghosts: "Sometimes the banshee assumes the form of some sweet singing virgin of the family who died young, and has been given the mission by the invisible powers to become the harbinger of coming doom to her mortal kindred. Or she may be seen at night as a shrouded woman, crouched beneath the trees, lamenting with veiled face; or flying past in the moonlight, crying bitterly: and the cry of this spirit is mournful beyond all other sounds on earth, and betokens certain death to some member of the family whenever it is heard in the silence of the night."[37]

Banshees are so attached to the families they protect that they accompany them wherever they go, even to foreign countries. The banshee of the O'Gradys, a family who emigrated to Canada, emitted long plaintiff cries when two members of their clan died in that far-off land.

BANSHEES PLAY CHESS

According to Sir Walter Scott, Scottish clans were also placed under the protection of a banshee, whose functions were even more important than in Ireland: "Several families of the Highlands of Scotland anciently laid claim to the distinction of an attendant spirit who performed the office of the Irish banshee.

"Amongst them, however, the functions of this attendant genius, whose form and appearance varied in different cases, were not limited to announcing the dissolution of those whose days were numbered. The Highlanders

Painting (left) :
Three women and three wolves, *Eugène Grasset (1841–1917), watercolour,* © Giraudon/Bridgeman *Art Library*

36 and 37. F. S. Wilde, *Ancient Legends of Ireland*, London, 1887.

contrived to exact from them other points of service, sometimes as warding off dangers of battle; at others, as guarding and protecting the infant heir through the dangers of childhood; and sometimes as condescending to interfere even in the sports of the chieftain, and point out the fittest move to be made at chess, or the best card to be played at any other game."[38]

In support of his claims, Scott cites the case of one of his ancestors who had one of these devoted phantoms in his service: "Among those spirits who have deigned to vouch their existence by appearance of late years, is that of an ancestor of the family of MacLean of Lochbuy. Before the death of any of this race, the phantom-chief gallops along the sea-beach near to the castle, announcing the event by cries and lamentations. The spectre is said to have rode his rounds and uttered his death-cries within these few years, in consequence of which the family and clan, though much shocked, were in no way

surprised to hear by next accounts that their gallant chief was dead at Lisbon, where he served under Lord Wellington."[39]

In the Scottish Highlands, a banshee nicknamed "the little washer by the ford" laundered the clothing of those who were to perish in battle. Each morning, the MacLeod banshee would hoist the flag bearing the family coat of arms, and rock the infant heir in his crib. During the seventeenth century, the Grant clan's banshee would tell his master the winning moves at chess.

Centaurs

Centaurs are half-man, half-horse creatures from Greek mythology, with the lower body of a horse and the head and torso of a man. They lived in Thessaly and later in the Peloponnese archipelago.

The most celebrated, Chiron, was renowned for his wisdom, and was the instructor of the hero Hercules.

In the *Metamor-* *phoses*, Ovid recounts the war waged by the centaurs on the people of the Lapithes. King Pirithous had invited the centaurs to his marriage to make peace with them; but the "horse men" became inebriated, started a fight and carried off all the women present, including the queen herself! During the combat which ensued many centaurs were slain.

Displaying characteristics of strength, lubricity and a taste for wine, centaurs have only two gods: Eros, god of Love, and Dionysus, god of wine and intoxication.

38 and 39. Walter Scott, *Histoire de la démonologie et de la sorcellerie*, translation by M. Defauconpret, Furne Éditeur, Paris, 1832.

White Ladies

Always dressed in white, these ladies are sometimes considered as kindly and mischievous, and sometimes as the ghosts of noble castle mistresses who died under tragic circumstances; they return to their former homes to protect their descendents or to warn them of their imminent passing, like the banshees of Ireland and Scotland.

In Germany, Dame Bertha was a White Lady who appeared at the birth of heirs of princely families. She also announced the death of rulers, and was seen on the keep of various castles in Germany and Bohemia. According to Erasmus, a White Lady was to be seen in Germany whenever death was about to strike a prince or a lord: "This spectre has appeared since the earliest times in the noble homes of Neuhaus and Rosenberg, and still shows itself there today."[40] These White Ladies or "Dames" also exist in France, where they have given their name to different localities such as le Chemin des Dames, la Combe aux Dames, le Pré aux Dames, la Cour des Dames or le Banc des Dames.

Malesherbes recounts how, on the day prior to the sentencing of Louis XVI, the monarch asked him if he had seen the White Lady who traditionally appeared around the *Palais des Bourbons* to announce the death of a prince. Similarly, a White Lady swept the floors of the castle whenever misfortune was about to strike

the Hohenzollern family.[41] The White Lady of the Habsbourgs usually dwelt in the Hofburg, and appeared each time a member of the imperial family was about to die. She was also seen at Yute, in the Spanish monastery where Charles the Fifth lay agonising, as well as at Mayerling on the eve of the

The appearance of the White Lady always foretells the death of a ruler

*Illustration:
© Sandrine Gestin*

40. Erasmus, *Des Prodiges.*
41. Cited by Éloïse Mozzani, *Magie et superstitions de la fin de l'Ancien Régime à la Restauration*, Robert Laffont, 1988.

The nymph "keeps her distance once again", *Thomas Cooper Gotch (1854–1931), watercolour, © Giraudon/Bridgeman Art Library*

42. A. de Chesnel, *Dictionnaire des superstitions, erreurs, préjugés et traditions populaires où sontexposées les croyances superstitieuses des temps anciens and modernes,* tome XX of *L'Encyclopédie théologique,* 1856.

drama which was to unfold. Being usually well intentioned, these White Ladies are often to be found near wayside chapels. They direct erring travellers to the correct path, bring food to lonely shepherds or accompany children lost in the woods. There was once a White Lady who lived near a stream close to Antwerp: "She was a very kindly person who consoled children and gave them the means to help their parents."[42] They may also appear in stables. In their hands they hold lighted candles, letting the melted wax drop onto the horses' manes, before brushing and plaiting them.

Other times, alas, for their simple amusement, these White Ladies lead passers-by to the edge of

cliffs and push them over, having no regard for their fate. More recently, White Ladies have taken on the appearance of phantom hitchhikers who appear to motorists on the roadside, usually at spots where a fatal accident has occurred. Many reports have been gathered from various places over more than two decades which appear to confirm the ongoing activity of these ghosts, whom eyewitnesses consider as fulfilling the role of a protector.

Dryads

Dryads are nymphs who preside over the woods and especially oak trees. They resemble very beautiful young girls whose arms and legs are shaped like arabesques, thus imitating the trunk of a tree. They embody the vegetative powers of the forests. Unlike the hamadryads, who inhabit one tree in particular, dryads roam freely, dancing in circles around oak trees, and they may even marry humans. Eurydice was a dryad when

she wed Orpheus. While not immortal, dryads can live a very long time.

HAMADRYADS

Hamadryads are wood nymphs who are born and die with the same tree, unlike the dryads, who survive beyond the destruction of their protégés. Ovid tells of the sad fate of a hamadryad condemned to die because of Erysichton's axe: "I am a nymph who is dear to Ceres. I live in this tree and I am dying because of your crime. The heavens will avenge me: the punishment which is reserved for you, and which I shall announce to you when I perish shall make my shadow rejoice on the night I die."[43] But the man was obstinate, and cut down the oak in which the nymph lived. "The horrified dryads wept for their lost sister, and the forest grieved for her despoiled honour. They clad themselves in funerary garb and trembling before Ceres, they begged him to make sure that Erysichton received a punishment worthy of his impiety."[44]

Goblins

Fadets, fradets, frérots, follets, foulets, ferrés, fols, furseys, folatons (France); foletti, farfarelli (Italy); bouquins (Wales); caraquins (Scotland); perchevins (Isle of Man)

Goblins are the elfish spirits of the forest, and while their name is derived from "fade" meaning "fairy", they have very little in common with the fairies.

Towards the end of the nineteenth century, the valley of Egray, near Germond in the Deux-Sèvres district, was considered the exclusive domain of the goblins, who did not like being disturbed by the women who gathered there in caves or quarries to spin their yarn. When returning to the village in the evenings, they would see the goblins charging up the winding road at breakneck speeds in an enormous chariot with creaking wheels. Then one of the spinners had the idea of making the sign of the cross, after which both goblins and chariot disappeared instantly.

Like imps, who are sometimes confused with goblins, the latter very readily take to horses, are generally good with them, and delight in curling and tangling their manes. It is difficult to describe them for they are mostly invisible, unless they take on the appearance of animals.

However, they were observed by Brian Froud and Alan Lee: "The goblin is a shabby, wrinkled little fellow, with a swarthy complexion, a half-metre tall, who roams about naked or dressed in tattered brown. The mountain goblins have neither fingers nor toes, and the plain-dwellers have no nose."[45]

While his natural habitat is some molehill in the forest, the goblin sometimes adopts the role of a servant spirit and then takes up residence in a house or a farm. In such cases, he looks after the animals and the housework, reaps and threshes the harvest, and finishes off all those tasks that the servants and worker have

Fadets, fradets, frérots, folleta, fouleta, ferrés, fols, furseys, folatons, foletti, farfarelli, bouquins, caraquins, perchevins

Illustrations: © Sandrine Gestin

43 and 44. Ovide, *Métamorphoses*, book VIII, translation by G. T. Villenave.
45. Brian Froud and Allan Lee, *Les Fées*, Albin Michel, 1979.

de Plancy tells the following tale: "In the year 1221, around harvest time, the friar in the kitchen of a monastery at Citeaux ordered two servants to guard the grapevines during the night. One night, feeling very sleepy, one of the men called to the devil in a loud voice and promised to pay him well if he would guard the vines in his place. Hardly had he uttered these words when a goblin appeared.

"'Here I am, ready and willing,' he said to the sleepy one. 'What will you give me in exchange for my trouble?'

"'I'll give you a basketful of grapes,' replied the manservant, 'and good ones at that, but only if you keep watch until morning.'

"The goblin accepted the offer, and the servant returned to the house to rest. The kitchen friar, who was still up, asked why he had left the vineyard.

"'My companion is keeping watch,' he replied, 'and he will guard it well.'

"'Go, go,' replied the cook, unaware of what was happening, 'your companion might need your help.'

"The manservant dared not answer back and went out, but took care not to go back to the vineyard. He called the other manservant and told him what he had done. Counting on the goblin guarding the vines, both men crept into a small cave nearby and went to sleep. Everything went according to plan; the faithful goblin remained at his post until morning, and he was given the basket of grapes as promised."[47]

not had time to complete – but not before punishing them for their laziness or their negligence by giving them a sound whack with a stick.

For all these services the goblin asks only a trifling salary: "In exchange for his labour, the goblin wishes for nothing more than a bowl of cream or fresh milk with a honey cake. Should one wish to offer him more, he becomes offended and runs away, which often happens when the master of the house demonstrates misplaced generosity by leaving out new clothing for the goblin."[46] He then exclaims:

Hemp, hee! [Hemp, hi!
What's here, a rough hemp shirt [I spy!
So never more work nor dwell here [shall I!

GOBLINS AND THE MONASTERY

Those little rascal goblins were also in the habit of haunting monasteries. Collin

THE SCOURGE OF THE GOBLINS

In 1821, a certain Alexis Vincent Charles Berbiguier from Terre-Neuve du Thym (1776–1852), a native of Carpentras, published an enormous work in three volumes, in which the author, who almost certainly suffered from mythomania and galloping paranoia, tried to pass off goblins as demons who had come from hell with the sole aim of tormenting him.

A bowl of cream and some honey cake are the goblin's only wages

46. Brian Froud and Allan Lee, *Les Fées*, Albin Michel, 1979.
47. Collin de Plancy, *Dictionnaire infernal*, 1825–1826.

He wrote: "These cheeky little devils go about at night surprising the ladies, or even sneak invisibly into their beds, use magnetism to lull them to sleep, and by a goblinesque procedure they bring into the world a bastard or adulterine infant."[48] According to Berbiguier, this same fate could await widows and spinsters, who observed their bellies grow large without knowing the cause of it, until such time as they brought into the world the "fruit of their goblinesque pleasure". Having resolved to take up the cause of these innocent "goblinised victims", Berbiguier wrote a dedication in his work urging all emperors, kings and sovereign princes to join with him in fighting "to destroy the influence of demons, sorcerers and goblins" who were harming the inhabitants of their states: "Ah! This diabolical persecution by the goblins would have ended long ago on Earth if only some of your subjects had shown the courage to denounce them."[49]

Fauns

Goat's-feet, égipans, satyrs, silenes (ageing satyrs), serim (hairy demons in the Old Testament), woodland elves

In Roman antiquity, fauns were rustic divinities and companions of the god Faunus, protector of animals and shepherds.

Fauns are depicted as having hairy bodies like a deer, with long pointy ears, eyes slanting upwards, and with the horns and hooves of a goat. They resemble satyrs, but their features are less hideous; they have a more pleasant face, and are not so cruel.

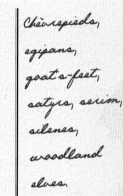

Chèvrepieds, égipans, goat's-feet, satyrs, serim, silenes, woodland elves.

48 and 49.
A. Berbiguier, *Le Fléau des farfadets, ou tous les démons ne sont pas de l'autre monde*, 1821.

According to Plutarch, in the time of Sylla (138–78 BC), a faun was found near Apollonia, the ancient city of Illyria. "This faun could utter no words at all; his voice was nothing more than a wild, harsh cry sounding like something between the whinny of a horse and the bleat of a goat. He showed little interest in the company of men although much interest in that of women."[50]

This propensity for gracing women with their presence caused the fauns, alongside satyrs, to be classed as incubi by theologians and demonologists, based on the opinion of Saint Augustine, who confirmed the existence of "fauns, these lewd disturbers of conjugal nights".[51]

WOODLAND ELVES AND GOAT'S FEET

The woodland elves live with their female companions in the woods and forests. They closely resemble fauns, satyrs and goat's-feet.

Their god, Sylvain, son of Saturn or Faunus, has similar characteristics to the god Pan. He is depicted as a jolly old fellow endowed with the horns, hooves and ears of a billy-goat. The god of fertility, nature, the woods and the fields, he is also considered to be an incubus who terrorises women in childbirth and children.

As for the goat's-feet, they are men with a goat's head and hooves. These small deformed creatures had one or two horns instead of hair. In reality, goat's-feet are a type of woodland elf, faun or satyr. It is sometimes said that the flute-playing god Pan, a familiar of the satyrs who caused nymphs and shepherds to throw fits of panic, was a goat's-feet.

BEWARE OF SATYRS!

While satyrs look rather similar to the Latin fauns, they are uglier and wilder, and represent rustic

divinities of Greek Antiquity. These hairy men with the horns, ears, tail, thighs and hooves of a goat, also have virile organs of impressive dimensions. They associate with the god Pan and go hunting nymphs, which they court in the

woods. Failing to catch any, they turn their attentions to young maidens or boys who cross their path. Herodotus spoke of a variety of satyrs, called egipans, living in the mountains of Scythia. As they grow older and wiser, satyrs are known as silenes.

The naturalist Pliny turned some into a type of monkey which terrified shepherds in the mountains in India. Saint Jerome declared that satyrs were the fruit of unions between men and goats. Saint Anthony met

50. Gratien de Semur,
Traité des erreurs et des préjugés, Paris,
A. Levasseur, 1843.
51. Collin de Plancy,
Dictionnaire infernal,
1825–1826.

Salacious lubriques satyrs were considered to be devils by the Church

one in the desert who was an ambassador of the satyr people, and who offered him dates in exchange for his prayers of intercession to the Lord. From the Middle Ages until the Renaissance, the Church went to great pains to identify these pagan creatures with demons who "in the name of Bacchanalia, formerly participated in drunken midnight revelry on Mount Parnassus. They appeared in groups, carrying cymbals and drums; their voices were human and clearly articulated, and one never knew from which side of the mountain they would come, for it had never been acknowledged that there were such inhabitants on that mountain. But was it something other than demons who came to the ceremonies and homages offered by magicians in the form of satyrs, and in the name of religion? It is said they still do so today at nocturnal assemblies of witches, called sabbaths, in order to indulge in their dances and their depraved activities."[52]

Collin de Plancy reports the following eyewitness account: "The Marshall of Beaumanoir was hunting in a forest in the Maine district in 1599,

when his attendants brought him a man whom they had found asleep under a bush. He had the strangest face, with two horns on his temples which were shaped and placed just like a ram. He was bald, and on his chin he had a sparse red beard, like those we see in paintings of satyrs. He became so distressed from being trundled from fair to fair that he died in Paris within three months. He was buried in the cemetery of Saint-Côme."[53]

Fairies

Fata, fades, fadas, fayes, fays, fairies (Great Britain), bonnes dames, gentes demoiselles, féetauds (masc.) (France)

Fairies are marvellous feminine creatures endowed with supernatural powers. They are generally good and have the ability to grant wishes to mortals, protect them, and even bestow talents on newborns simply by

leaning over their cribs. But they can also be evil and destructive, acting more like witches.

In the Middle Ages they were depicted as beautiful, tall and slender, richly dressed women. From the time of Shakespeare's fairy Mab, down to Walt Disney's Tinkerbell, they have become minute little creatures with wings on their backs like dragonflies or butterflies. Nowadays they are hardly ever seen for more than the twinkling of an eye. The only time when they are commonly seen, if you know their hiding places, is on the first of May, the Celtic feast day of Beltaine.

Fairies live in the kingdom of Fairy land, which is governed sometimes by the tiny Queen Mab, and at others by Queen Titania, wife of Oberon. They also live on enchanted isles such as the mythical Avalon, governed by the fairy Morgana, where the apples of immortality and eternal youth grow.

Some eyewitnesses have testified to the existence of male fairies, or féetauds, but these are in the minority, and they have far fewer powers than

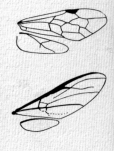

52. François Hedelin, *Des satyres, brutes, monstres et démons*, Paris, 1627.

53. Collin de Plancy, *Dictionnaire infernal*, 1825–1826.

Pretty fairies with butterfly wings appear on Mayday, the feast day of Beltaine

*Painting (right):
Iris, the fairy, (detail)
1886, John Atkinson
Grimshaw (1836–1893),
oil on canvas,
© Giraudon/Bridgeman
Art Library*

their sisters and partners. Nor are they reported in the fairy tale literature.

WHERE DO THEY COME FROM?

The word "fairy" dates from the twelfth century, and comes from the Latin *fata*, derived from *fatum*, "destiny", *fata* in Italian, *fada* in Provençal and Languedoc, and *fade* in certain regions of France (Auvergne). The word "fairy" may also be derived from the Latin *fari*, "prophecy", which gives the Old French *faer*, "to enchant or charm" and *faé*, "enchanted", and fairy or fay in English.

Traditionally they are not directly named, but referred to by various gallant euphemisms such as "good dames" or "young maidens".

There are several theories to explain their origins. According to the Greeks and Romans, fairies descended from the Greek Moires, the Roman Parcae or fates, and the Nordic Nornes. That is why they are usually found in threes. The *fata* are tiny mythological divinites associated with tree, water and fountain cults. This cult of the forest fairies was passed to the Gauls at the time of the Roman invasion.

In Celtic folklore, fairies are the descendents of the druidesses responsible for cults. Like the ancient priestesses, fairies are often shown wearing white robes and a crown. The druidesses became goddesses of nature, especially of the forest. "They live in gloomy dens deep in the forest; sometimes they show themselves, they speak with whoever consults them, and are given to fainting suddenly."[54]

The courtly literature of the Middle Ages, which developed

Illustrations: © Sandrine Gestin

54. Olaüs Magnus, cited by Collin de Plancy, *Dictionnaire infernal*, 1825–1826.

out of the stories of King Arthur, gradually adopted the fairy in the guise of a lady who was beloved by her knight. The fairy-druidess thus became the fairy-princess.

For the cabalists and alchemists of the sixteenth century, fairies are the guardians of nature, especially trees and flowers. "While they were generous to mankind, good fairies were also the charming guardians of nature. They did their spring-cleaning by shaking from their dresses sinister deformed beasts. They brought calm to the raging elements and made peace reign in the hearts of mankind."[55]

During the seventeenth and eighteenth centuries in the literary salons and the court of the kings of France, the fairy appeared in folk tales, with a crown and a magic wand as symbols of her power. It was this enhanced image of the fairy godmother which made the French story books of Perrault, Mme d'Aulnoy or Mme Leprince of Beaumont so successful. A popular edition of these tales, which included Galland's *The Thousand and One Nights,* was published between 1785 and 1789 under the title *Le Cabinet des fées.* These "fairy tales" were initially designed for educated adult readers at the royal court, and were later adapted for juvenile literature.

THE FAIRY TRINITY

Fairies generally go in threes, like the spinners of fate: the Greek Moires, the Roman Parcae and the Nordic Nornes. Each fairy had a specific function: the first knotted the thread of human life by being present at birth, the second unwound it by intervening in the person's fate, and the third cut the thread by announcing imminent death, and accompanying the deceased to the realm of eternal youth beyond. The fairy's main role is to predict the future. But she not only announces it; she also decides and influences it as she sees fit, or according to orders from her superiors. She is the fairy godmother who leans over the newborn babe in his crib and endows him with gifts, as we read in all the fairy tales.

Fairies are also magicians. They participate in man's destiny, working a thousand wonders and supernatural events, sometimes for his benefit and sometimes to his misfortune.

And finally the fairy announces the death of men and accompanies them when they depart this life. This one is the "wicked" or "forgotten fairy" in tales such as *The Sleeping Beauty,* where the fairy predicts that the heroine will prick her finger with a needle at the age of sixteen and fall into a sleep as deep as death. Another was Morgana, queen of the enchanted isle of Avalon, who took King Arthur to this Celtic

The first knots the thread of life, the second unwinds it, and the third cuts it

55. Henri Durville, *Les Fées*, Perthuis, 1950.

paradise when he was mortally wounded, and cared for him by letting him taste the apples of eternal youth. Then there was Keats' "Belle Dame Sans Merci", that deadly fairy who seduced a knight-errant in a secret valley. But when he bent to kiss her, she drew out his breath and his soul in a kiss of death.

FAIRY RINGS

One of the surest signs that fairies are to be found in a forest is the "fairy ring" they leave behind after dancing there for many long hours: "When picking daisies you will often find them on grassy hillsides, in a circular patch of grass which is taller, greener and more lush than elsewhere. These rings may be full or only semicircles of varying diameters and widths, which seem to have been traced with a compass; in autumn they turn crimson with a crown of fairy toadstools and other brightly coloured cryptic symbols. An old

tradition says that fairies danced there in the moonlight."[56] The folklore specialist Evans Wentz writes: "The grass never grows high on the edges of these rings because there it is shorter and finer. In the centre are toadstools which the fairies

sit on. These tiny people love to dance and sing."[57] It can be very dangerous to walk into one of these fairy rings, because he who does will be swept up in their dancing, and forced to continue until he falls totally exhausted, or even dies. It is

also said that in Fairyland time passes differently than for humans; the dance seems to last for only a few minutes, but in reality it lasts several days, years or even centuries.

THE FAIRY LOVER

The fairy lover first appeared in tales during the Middle Ages, and then became the heroine of the tales of chivalry. Often while pursuing some fabulous game, such as a pure white doe, stag or boar, the proud knight is lead unawares to an enchanted palace where the fairy awaits, and makes him a prisoner of love. So he is transformed from the hunter into the prey, tormented by his passion for this *belle dame*, who enslaves him and makes him her knight-in-waiting.
This exceedingly beautiful fairy lover uses all her charms to make a man fall in love and marry her, thus ensuring that the line will continue. But this union with the fairy is always based on one essential condition, some-

A fairy minute lasts a century for humans.

56. Stanislas de Guaita, *Le Temple de Satan*, 1915.
57. W.Y. Evans Wentz, *The Fairy-Faith in Celtic Countries*, 1911.

The fairy Melusine accepted to wed Raymondin on condition that he would never try to see her on Saturdays, which she reserved for bathing. The lord respected this taboo for several years, until one day, influenced by his brother, he thrust his sword through the door behind which his wife was bathing. In fact, Melusine had a spell upon her which transformed her lower body into a serpent's tail. On hearing his cries of horror, Melusine knew that Raymondin had broken his promise. In an instant, she changed into a winged snake and flew out the window, never to return.

THE BLACKSMITH AND THE GOOSE-FOOTED FAIRY

The fact that humans were usually disloyal to their fairy wives caused them to avoid the company of mortals, which in turn hastened the fairies' exile, as this anecdote illustrates:

"A lady from the fairy grotto of Vallorbe agreed to take a blacksmith as her husband, but made him promise that he would see her only when she felt it was appropriate to show herself, and that he would never follow her into another part of

thing that is taboo or forbidden, that most mortals are unable to keep for very long. If he breaks the rules even once, his fairy-tale wife leaves forever, taking her babes far away to Fairyland.

FAIRY TABOOS

The most common taboos imposed by fairies are that you must not call them by name, remind them of their supernatural origins, reveal their existence to others, use certain words or phrases in their presence, beat them, take them on water or touch them with metal objects.

bed, and beneath her skirts he saw what looked exactly like a goose's feet! Awakened by the yapping of her little dog, the fairy chased him from the grotto and threatened him with the most dreadful punishment if he ever told what he had seen. The blacksmith could not help but tell his friends what he had seen, and as proof, he showed them two purses that the fairy had given him. But in the one which had contained gold coins, all he found was a few willow leaves, and in the other where before there were pearls, now there were only juniper berries. At the same time, the fairies disappeared: it was said that they had gone into hiding in the deepest caves of Montcherand near Orta, but no-one ever dared go inside to see if this was really true."[58]

FAIRY COOKING

In his famous work *Traité de Faërie*, Ismaël Mérindol explains that fairies do not eat substantial food, but prefer delicacies such as food smells, various essences, threads of cloud, the stuff of dreams, the air of time, the colours of the seasons and morning dew. But they do love treats such as freshly picked juniper berries, flower stamens, cow's milk, butter, honey and saffron.

milk, butter and saffron are the fairies' favourite foods

CHANGELINGS

Fairies sometimes steal unbaptised babies, and replace them with their own, known as "changelings". Paul Sébillot reports that "fairies steal infants they like and substitute their own, which are usually rather ugly and wizened; in some areas, and especially in Brittany, children who look like this are known as a 'fairy's child.'"[59]

To get rid of the changeling, you must make it speak and tell how old it is. Usually it is of a certain age, because fairies' children are born old.

the cave other than where they had first met. All was well for fifteen days, but on the sixteenth, while the fairy was in another room taking a nap, her husband opened the door just a crack. His wife was resting on the

58 and 59. Paul Sébillot, *Croyances, mythes et légendes des pays de France, Le Monde Souterrain*, (1904–1906), Omnibus, 2002.

The best way is to surprise it by doing something really strange, such as mixing beer with eggshells, or arranging a collection of pots, pans, and pitchers full of boiling liquid around its crib. The changeling will then cry:

I am more than two hundred and ten,
I saw the acorn before the oak,
I saw the egg before the hen,
But never have I seen so many
[little boiling pans!

With that, the changeling flies up the chimney with a sneering laugh, and the human baby resumes its normal place in the cradle. This anecdote illustrates the best way to get rid of overpowering changelings: "A dazzlingly beautiful fairy lived in a cave in the valley of Réchanté with her son who was sickly, hump-backed and mute as well; she carried off one of the prettiest children in the village, leaving her own child at the foot of a tree. Two caring young girls found him there and took him home, but despite all their care he did not thrive. An old woman advised the family to gather as many eggshells as they could and place them around the hearth in front of a large fire. They did this, sitting the little fellow on a wooden stool nearby. At the sight of so many eggshells, the dwarf, who had never so much as uttered one word until then, cried out: '*Té vu tre cou prà, tre cou tchan, tre cou arbrou gran, e jamé vu tan dé ballerot otor dou fouec.*' 'I have seen three meadows, three fields, and three huge forests, but never have I seen so many play-things around a fireplace.' Then the old woman told the parents of the stolen child to take the dwarf to the cave and whip him soundly. Hearing the screams of her child, the fairy ran to her son's aid, while the parents hurried into the grotto and snatched up their son."[60]

In *Traité de Faërie*, Mérindol reveals that he himself was a changeling, who was raised by a foster family in a small village in Provence, early in the fifteenth century. Like all children of fairies, he was born old and full of fairy wisdom. Soon he left home and went to study in various universities of Europe, finally settling in Prague. After leaving this world he came back as a fairy in 1522, at the age of one hundred and twenty in human years.

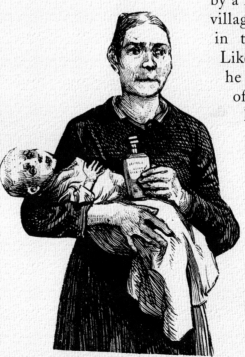

60. Paul Sébillot, *Croyances, mythes et légendes des pays de France, Le Monde Souterrain*, (1904–1906), Omnibus, 2002.

Painting (left):
Portrait of the Italian
composer Cherubini
(1760–1842) with the muse
of lyric poetry, *1842, Jean
Auguste Dominique Ingres
(1780–1867), oil on canvas,*
© *Giraudon/Bridgeman
Art Library*

Are the muses simply good fairies?

In Greek mythology, the muses are the daughters of Zeus and
Mnemosyne, the goddess of Memory. Nine in all, they preside over
the arts and sciences: Clio for history, Euterpe for music, Thalia for
comedy, Melpomene for tragedy, Terpsichore for dance, Erato for
elegy, Polymnia for lyric poetry, Urania for astronomy and
Calliope for eloquence and heroic poetry. They lived with Apollo,
Parnassus, Pindar and Helicon. ❧

*The muses
provide
inspiration
for poets and
artists*

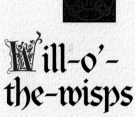

Will-o'-the-wisps

Ignis fatuus, Jack o' lantern, Will-o'-the-wisp (England), pwca, pooka (Wales), feux follets (France), folletti (Italy)

*Ignis fatuus,
Jack with the
lantern, Will
o' the wisp,
pwca, pooka*

*Illustration:
© Sandrine Gestin*

Will-o'-the-wisps appear in the form of small flames, fireballs or phosphorescence which glows in the dark, especially during Advent, in dense forests, near graveyards or hovering over marshlands. Like sprites, who come from the goblin family, will-o'-the-wisps are lost souls praying for release from purgatory, the souls of unbaptised infants, or wicked spirits who are trying to lead travellers into ponds or to the edges of cliffs.

In the Landes district, the ghost of the priest of Commensacq, Abbey Ducasse, appeared in 1822 on a path just outside the village, in a surplice and cape. But this was no illusion: "This path ran beside a marsh, and the people considered the will-o'-the-wisps which hovered regularly over the marshes were ghosts."[61]

At Pont-Audemer in Northern France, will-o'-the-wisps assumed the form of women who had sinned during their lives, and who were condemned to come back in that form for seven years.

In Wales, they are spirits who have come in search of a relative who is about to die, with the size of the flame corresponding to the age of the person on their death bed: thus a tiny will-o'-the-wisp announces the death of a child.

In England they are also called jack-o'-lantern. These *ignis fatuus*, or fire spirits, are represented as young boys carrying lanterns, who lead lost travellers to the edge of dangerous precipices. Then they snuff out their candle and the unfortunate victim goes over the edge. In Wales, this sinister game is played by a character known as pwca, or pooka, a lively imp who gets up to all sorts of mischief.

HOW TO GET RID OF THEM

All you need do is cross yourself or stick a needle into some earth. The will-o'-the-wisp must slip through the eye, and this gives you the opportunity you need to escape. To flee from will-o'-the-wisps in ponds all you need do is throw a stone into the water. Persuaded that they have accomplished what they intended, the will-o'-the-wisps run off into the shadows sneering gleefully.

61. V. Foix, *Auch*, 1904.

The water people

-3-

*T*he water people are mainly female: mermaids with enchanting voices, Mari Morgan with blonde hair, fertile freshwater nymphs, ondines who bathe naked in rivers, rebellious spring naiads, and lake-dwelling nixies who cast spells. These aquatic creatures are sensual lovers, who think only of seducing mortals and carrying them down to their underwater palaces. But often their love is deadly, and a number of men who frequented these water maids sacrificed their health, their lives and even their souls. To say nothing of the unfortunate victims of the terrible night washerwomen, wivres with the tail of a snake, cruel groac'hs *and other water witches.*

SEA CREATURES

Mari Morgan

Mari Morgan are water fairies from Brittany, who look just like women. They are never found in the open seas, but close to shore, near the entrance to caves or at river mouths. The folklore specialist, Paul Sébillot, writes: "These brazen ones are well versed in the science of evil, pursuing young fishermen for love: those they managed to seduce were carried underwater and never seen again."[62]

Mari Morgan drag their lovers, usually sailors, down to their sumptuous underwater palaces and hold them prisoner there eternally. In Brittany it is said that these kingdoms are like whole countries, with countryside, mountains, orchards and gardens. The castles are decorated with garlands of seaweed and coral. The residents and visitors to these ocean depths never want for air or light, and visibility is almost like on land. The fish swim back and forth between the seabed and the surface, carrying air in their mouths which they expel, thus forming gigantic bubbles to supply the aquatic kingdom, along the lines of a huge diving bell.

Innumerable Breton sailors have given in to the seduction of the Mari Morgan, and followed them to their mother-of-pearl and crystal palaces, where they can indulge themselves in all sorts of pleasures. They married Mari Morgan, had many offspring, and adapted so well to their sub mariners' life that they forgot completely about their existence on land.

MARI MORGAN OF THE CROZON CAVE

"Even today there are Mari Morgan living in a cave near Crozon, which is often inaccessible because of the sea. One evening a lord, who regretted having no children, found a pretty little girl aban-doned in a reed basket on the path leading to his castle. He took her home to his wife and they brought her up as their daughter. But she was a Mari Morgan: often at night the child would disappear from her cot and no-one ever knew where she went. When she grew older, horses' hooves could often be heard in the castle courtyard: a 'folgoat' was calling for the Mari Morgan. A bright light flashed: it was the young girl answering this call. She would go, and sometimes be away for weeks at a time. Her family tried in vain to hold her back; then one day she left, never to return. The locals swear that she still lives in that cave, which is the last of the Mari Morgan dwellings."[63]

*Illustration:
© Sandrine Gestin*

62 and 63. Paul Sébillot, *Croyances, mythes et légendes des pays de France, La Mer*, (1904–1906), Omnibus, 2002.

Illustration:
© Sandrine Gestin

Morgans and morganes

Mermen (masc. in English), morganed (masc. in Breton), morganès (fem.), morganezed (fem. plural)

Morgans and morganes – which are distinct from Mari Morgan – are graceful elves who live on the Isle of Ouessant.
In 1873, Marie Tual, a native of Ouessant, gave the following description of the folklore specialist François-Marie Luzel: "Morganed and morganezed are little, rosy-cheeked men and women with curly blond hair and shining big blue eyes; they are as sweet as angels. Unfortunately they have never been baptised, and for this reason they can never go to heaven, which is a pity, given that they are such beautiful and good people!"[64]
She continued: "Morganed and morganezed used to be commonly seen on our island; nowadays we rarely see them because we treated them so badly. They can be seen in the moonlight, sporting and frolicking in the fine sand and the seaweed on the shore, combing their blond tresses with combs of ivory and gold.

Morganed,
Morganès,
Morganezed

64 and 65. François-Marie Luzel, *Notes de voyage*, 1873, reprint, Terre de Brume, 1997.

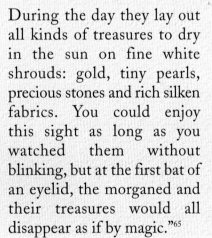

During the day they lay out all kinds of treasures to dry in the sun on fine white shrouds: gold, tiny pearls, precious stones and rich silken fabrics. You could enjoy this sight as long as you watched them without blinking, but at the first bat of an eyelid, the morganed and their treasures would all disappear as if by magic."[65]
Marie Tual tells many other marvellous tales about the morgans, including this one from Luzel: "I have heard it told that the Virgin Mary was at home alone one day, and needing to go and draw water from the well, she found herself in difficulty, as she did not wish to leave her newborn son, who was asleep in his crib. " 'What shall I do? The spring is quite a way off, and I cannot leave my child alone,' she said to herself.
"At that very moment she heard the soft, sweet voice of a child saying: 'I'll watch over him if you wish.'
"Turning, she saw on the doorstep a small man smiling so kindly that she thought for only a moment before deciding to leave him with the infant and go to fetch the water from the spring.
"When she returned, to thank the faithful guardian, she

asked him to make a wish and it would be granted.

"'Gened ha morgened,' which means: beauty and lots of little morgans, replied the little fellow.

"His wish was granted, and that is why morgans were so attractive and so plentiful in bygone days. But he would have been better off to ask for baptism, because then he and his kind would have gone to heaven with the angels, whom they resemble so closely."[66]

Oceanids, nereids

Oceanids are marine nymphs born from the incestuous union between the god Oceanus and his sister, Tethys. According to Hesiodus: "Tethys gave birth to a holy race of daughters spread across the Earth, who in turn raised children with the god Apollo and his rivers; this fate was decided for her by Zeus himself.

"Throughout the world there are about three thousand oceanids, these radiant children of goddesses with fine-shaped ankles, who watch over the Earth and the depths of the ocean."[67] Together the oceanids Doris and Nereus had fifty sea nymphs or nereids, who symbolise virtue and justice.

There are large numbers of nereids in the Mediterranean and the Aegean, personifying the motion of the waves and the various moods of the sea: Thalia, green; Glaucea, blue; Cymodocea, flowing like tears; Dynamene, raging; Cymodareus, becalmed. Like mermaids, the nereids have

66. François-Marie Luzel, *Notes de voyage*, 1873, reprint, Terre de Brume, 1997.

67. Hediod, *Theogony*.

Mermaids,
seraines,
serres

melodious voices which they use to please their father Nerea, and not to cause death to seafarers, whom they protect. They take on the appearance of sensual young ladies astride dolphins or seahorses, their hair threaded with pearls.

Pliny the Elder described them thus: "The shape of nereids is not imaginary. But their bodies are covered with scales, even on the human parts. In fact, one was found dying, and the locals could hear her mournful wails from afar."[68]

Selkies

Selkies are seal-women from the seas around the Shetland Isles. They wear sealskins to dive to the bottom of the ocean, and remove them when they are on land. Then they take on the form of

appealing young girls who spend the night dancing in the moonlight. But they must take care not to misplace their sealskins, because then they would not be able to return to their natural environment. Sometimes they only change their seal appearance once a year, and this is usually during the night of Saint-Jean, a magical night on which any sort of enchantment or metamorphosis is possible.

If a man manages to steal a selkie's sealskin, he can then control her. She stays with him and can even marry and bear his offspring. But the husband of a selkie must take great care to hide the sealskin, or better still burn it, for if she finds it she will slip it on, abandon her spouse and babes, and plunge back into the ocean.

Mermaids

Sirènes, seraines, serres

Mermaids look like women from the waist up, while the lower part of their body is a scaly fishtail. They live in the oceans and seas, and especially along rocky coast-

lines. As ships approach, they sing so sweetly that no mortal can resist the urge to follow them to their underwater domain, which has caused the death of many a sailor on the seas, and many shipwrecks. Their beauty and their fatal charms symbolise both seduction and the dangers of the sea.

Liber Monstrorum (Book of Monsters), an Anglo-Saxon

68. Pliny the Elder,
Historia naturalis.

manuscript dating from the eighth or ninth century, gives the following description: "Mermaids are young sea virgins who seduce sailors with their splendid bodies and their honeysweet melodies. From head to waist they are identical to women; but below they have a scaly fish's tail which they keep well hidden beneath the waves." Devotees of eroticism, art, music, singing and divination, these creatures are not immortal; nevertheless, according to Hesiodus they can live for up to 291,600 years in a state of perpetual youth.

WHERE DO THEY COME FROM?

The origin of mermaids is not known for certain, but they are said to be the daughters of the river Achelous, who is depicted as a fishtailed man, and one of the muses. The mythologist Gerhardt says it was most likely either Melpomenes, the muse of harmony; Terpsichore, muse of dancing; or Calliope, with the fine voice. Other writers affirm that they are the daughters of the goddess of Memory, Mnemosyne.

Claude Nicaise, the seventeenth-century writer, reports that they were born from the bleeding horn of plenty following Hercules' battle with Achelous: "Hercules had fought with Achelous over Dejanir. Achelous saw that he would be overpowered by the god, and wanting to avoid defeat at all costs, adopted many forms including that of a serpent and then a bull. Hercules tore off one of Achelous's horns, which was named the Horn of Plenty and given to Fortune as his constant companion. Achelous could not bear being deprived of one of his horns, so he gave Fortune another belonging to Amaltheus, and his own was returned to him. Finally conquered by the hero, he hid in the river which bears his name and which is shown with two horns. Poets say that mermaids were born from the blood of this horn wrenched out by Hercules."[69]

THEIR HOMES

At the tip of the Sorrento peninsula is a mermaid temple which, according to the ancients, was the residence of these maidens of the sea, situated on the rocks known as the Sirenuse islands. Quoting Aristotle: "The Sirenuse isles are said to be in Italy, at the entrance of a strait near a promontory surrounded by many bays, enclosing Cumes, and bordering on Poséidony (Positano). It is there that the mermaids' temple is located, and the local people paid homage with many sacrifices to these sites, called Parthenope, Leucosia and Ligea."

69. Claude Nicaise, *Discours sur les sirènes*, Paris, 1691.

However, Claude Nicaise considers that the mermaids live in the city of Naples: "We know that Naples was the place where the mermaids really lived, because where better could they be for all their pleasures, including their music, than in the city where the Roman emperors spent most of the year. I am convinced that the Neapolitans, being such fervent singers, have always taken Parthenope for their symbol."[70]

According to maritime legends, mermaids live in an underwater world in fabulous palaces to which they carry off their mortal lovers.

THE NAMES OF MERMAIDS AND THEIR MEANINGS

Aglaope: Beautiful, shining face.
Aglaophonos: Superb voice.
Leucosia: White creature.
Ligeia: Piercing scream.
Molpe: Singer of monotonous chants.
Parthenope: Face of a young maiden.
Peisinoe: Persuasive.
Raidne: Progressive.
Teles: Perfect.
Thelxinoe: Soother of souls with songs and music.

70. Claude Nicaise,
Discours sur les sirènes,
Paris, 1691.

Thelxiepia: She who utters soothing words.
Thelxiope: Convincing countenance.

CHARACTERISTICS OF MERMAIDS

The looking-glass: mermaids spend long periods gazing in their mirrors. Many consider that a sign of vanity, narcissism or coquetry. In fact, the mirror symbolises the planet Venus in astrology. Aphrodite, the Greek goddess of love, the arts and fertility, and born in the foamy brine, is often represented holding a mirror. Although she has no fish's tail, she is the ancestor of the mermaids and the protectress of seafarers.

Hair and golden combs: mermaids have long, thick tresses, symbolising sensual love. They spend their days tending their locks with golden combs, symbolising the female sex. The words *kteis* in Greek, *pectin* in Latin and *pettignone* in Italian mean both "comb" and "pubis". During the thirteenth century, the French word *séran* derived from *sirène* meant a comb which was used to card the tangled threads of flax or linen.

Ismaël Mérindol reveals that mermaids spend so much time combing their hair because that is their erogenous zone, and a source of incomparable pleasure. He writes: "In my youth I had a mermaid for a lover, but I was unable to give her pleasure in the usual way. However, if I scratched her scalp in a certain way she would very quickly swoon away. For what other women have between their legs, mermaids have in their hair."[71]

WINGED MERMAIDS

Their songs come from the fact that originally in Greek antiquity mermaids were not fish-women but bird-women with claws sometimes as strong as a lion's. These mermaids had the face of a young girl, but the claws and feathers of a bird. One of the reasons for this curious form is that Aphrodite punished them by changing them into birds because out of pride they had always refused to let a god or a man take their virginity. According to another legend, mermaids were the ladies in waiting of Proserpine, the daughter of Ceres. They allowed their mistress to be carried off by Pluto, who

71. Ismaël Mérindol, *Traité de Faërie*, 1466.

took her to hell. To punish the mermaids for their lack of vigilance, Ceres changed them into birds with women's heads. In his *Metamorphoses,* Ovid considers this rather to be an honour from the gods. Far from always being good, these mermaids of the air were known to swoop down like birds of prey on soldiers in battle or on sailors at sea.

HOW THE MERMAIDS LOST THEIR FEATHERS AND GAINED A FISHTAIL

The mermaids were to participate in a singing contest, pitted against the muses who brought them into the world. Hera was to judge this contest, in which the mermaids had the advantage, because of their sweeter voices. Refusing to admit defeat, the muses attacked the mermaids, tearing off their wings which they used to make crowns. No longer able to fly, the unfortunate mermaids sought refuge in the waves of the ocean. In the *Argonautica,* Apollonios of Rhodes tells the story of their defeat: "The mermaids sat on a snow-covered rock playing the flute and the lyre. They sighed at the thought of their impending

deadly fate, and so from the top of their rock they thrust themselves into the raging seas, where their bodies turned into stones."

But not all were changed into stones. The survivors, in the form of fish-women, went to live on shores or near coastal

reefs, watching out for sailors and seducing them with their song before taking them down to their underwater world. For mermaids are great romantics. In fact, as the saying goes, the reason the sea is so salty is that it is filled with the tears of lovesick mermaids.

mermaids are comforting for those destined to die: "Far from being inhumane and deadly, the singing of mermaids makes souls migrating from Earth to the other world forget all that is ephemeral and learn to love things divine. Their souls are captivated by this harmonious song, and follow it." The mermaid is not so much a demon lusting after souls, blood and sex, but rather a guardian angel. At this point the fish-woman is endowed with birds' wings, as in the Andersen fairy tale.

The mermaids' songs evoke sweet death and agonising pleasure

MERMAIDS' SONGS

In Homer's *Odyssey*, the reason why Ulysses was able to resist the mermaids' songs was because he followed the advice of the sorceress Circe, and lashed himself to the mast of his ship, while his sailors worked on board, their ears filled with wax. This mermaids' song is fatal for seamen, who are seduced by it; instantly losing their self-control, they throw themselves into the water and drown.

The cruel mermaids devour their hearts and steal their souls, leaving their drifting vessels to break up on the rocks. But such a horrible fate is considered to be pleasurable by their victims. Martial (40–103) speaks of the "hilarious suffering of sailors, that sweet death, that cruel pleasure". Claudanius (370–404) adds: "Their sacred music was an irresistible danger of the seas, and a pleasurable terror amidst the waves. The gentle wind played about the bow of the ship, while a voice resounded from the distance. The sailors refused to take the safe way home. Yet they did not suffer, for it was their joy that brought death." For Plutarch, the songs of

THE MEDIEVAL CLAWED MERMAID

The words "serene, Serena" are derived from the Latin *serra* or *siren*, meaning mermaid. During the Middle Ages, mermaids were commonly called "seraines" or "sirens", with reference to their sweet melodious songs. They were depicted in the bas-reliefs of Roman churches as symbols of lewd sexuality. Often they have forked fishtails which they hold apart with both hands, in lascivious poses. These mermaid temptresses embellish the ornamented capitals of manuscripts, as

well as shields and coats of arms, mosaics, stained glass, and holy-water stoups, as well as wooden and stone sculptures. Sometimes they wear a crown, or cradle an

infant in their arms. These Roman mermaids represent feminity, with all its grace and potential fertility, but also, in the eyes of the Church, its dangers and temptations. Richard of Fournival classified the different types of mermaid: "There are three types of mermaid, two of which are half woman and half fish, while the third is half woman and half bird. But all three are fine musicians: some play the trumpet, others the harp, and others sing. Their melody is so pleasant

that no man who hears them, however far he may be, can resist coming closer. When he is near, he drifts off to sleep, only to be killed by the waiting mermaid."[72]
The medieval bestiaries also mention a type of mermaid called a "serre", a woman with a fish's tail in the shape of the *fleur de lis*, with several wings sprouting from her wrists and elbows. The mermaid shown in the twelfth-century Cambridge Bestiary has a fishtail, cruel claws and a mixture of feathers and scales for a skirt. Symbolising the impure and lascivious woman, in Elizabethan England the mermaid was considered to be

a prostitute. According to Brunetto Latini, "Mermaids were three prostitutes who ensnared passers-by and reduced them to poverty. While history depicts them with wings and claws, this is to symbolise love, which is fleeting and inconstant; and they are always shown in water because lewdness is associated with moisture."[73]

FOUL WEATHER MERMAIDS

Sailors say that mermaids always mean bad weather. In Brittany, legend has it that seeing a naked mermaid, or inadvertently touching one, will cause a storm. Others believe that mermaids are able to take their victims down to their underwater palaces. The mermaid from Fort La Latte was responsible for the disappearance of many a young man. In South Finistere, everyone dreads the song of *"Mac'harit ar gwall amzer"* (Marguerite of the stormy weather), which is able to whip the sea into a fury. As the saying goes: "When Mac'harit sings the poor sailor sighs."

72. Richard de Fournival, *Bestiaire d'amour*, modern French edition by Gabriel Bianciotto, Stock/Moyen Âge, 1980.
73. Brunetto Latini, *Livre du trésor*, modern French edition by Gabriel Bianciotto, Stock/Moyen Âge, 1980.

In a folk song from the Poitou region, a young woman weeps for her lover, who has been seduced by a mermaid:

There is no fish or carp
Who has not wept for him.
There is but the mermaid
Who has always sung.
Sing, mermaid, sing,
As only you can;
For drink you have the brine
And my love to feast upon.[74]

MERMAID PROTECTORS

It was not until the Renaissance that mermaids lost their sinister reputation as prostitutes and demons, and finally became the protectors of sailors, their charming bodies embellishing maritime charts. In the midst of oceans was printed the following couplet: *Hic sunt sirenae* (The mermaids are here), alongside the coats of arms of ports and the bows of ships. They were the only females tolerated. Often they were coloured blue and gold, like madonnas. Similarly, Anglo-Saxon mermaids ("Virgins of the seas") are gentle creatures. Until the twentieth century, an English maritime law claimed for the Crown of

England "any mermaid found in English waters".

SAILORS AS EYEWITNESSES

From the fifteenth century on, during the times of the great seafaring expeditions, many seafarers' and sailors' reports seemed to confirm the existence of mermaids in the seas. Archbishop Bartolomé de Las Casas, who accompanied Christopher Colombus on several of his voyages, reported that the explorer who dis-

covered the Americas had seen mermaids: "On Wednesday, 9 January 1493, close to the isle of Santo Domingo, he saw three mermaids. They rose quite high out of the water. But he did not find them at all beautiful." The Jesuit Charlevoix (1682–1761) offered the probably valid explanation that these so-called mermaids were in fact sea-cows (now extinct), or cetaceans, with human-looking but ugly faces, three or four metres long. These creatures lived in the Caribbean, and the females had two large breasts; or perhaps they were dugongs, cetaceans with a flattened face, who live in the Indian and Red Seas. Spanish sailors called both sea-cows and dugongs "fish-women", because these two species emitted cries or lamentations (thus, the name *lamantin* in French) which sounded like human voices or the singing of mermaids.

THE GRATEFUL MERMAIDS

In Guernsey and in Brittany, many witnesses have seen these fish-women. An old man in Guernsey who was standing on the cliffs claimed to have seen a group of six

"In stormy weather, when Marguerite sings, the poor sailor sighs."

74. J. Bujeaud, *Chansons populaires de l'Ouest.*

mermaids lined up on the sea shore. He hurried down to inspect them more closely, but the timid mermaids disappeared beneath the waves. Another time, in the Bay of Fresnaye in Brittany, there was a mermaid whose melodious voice rang out and who left a silvery trail behind her. Paul Sébillot writes: "One day, with the gentle movement of the waves, she fell asleep, and was caught by a clog-maker, who threw her back into her natural element. To thank him, she endowed him with gifts. When she left Brittany for India, she gave his children a magic purse which was always full; another mermaid gave a flute to a young fisherboy who had put her back into the water, and she came to his aid whenever he played it."[75]
But you must never touch a mermaid's hair when putting her back in the water, or you will fall victim to her spell. In Vendee, a fisherman was about to return a mermaid to the sea when she warned him with the following words:
Take me in your arms. So long
[as you
Don't touch my head you needn't
[fear.
But, alas, your fingers will never
[be free
If ever they muss my golden
[hair!

75 and 76. Paul
Sébillot, *Croyances,*
mythes et légendes des
pays de France, la Mer,
(1904–1906), Omnibus,
2002.

I'll take you down, then, to my cave
[in the sea
Where forever there you'll dwell
[with me. [76]
Mermaids are always grateful when humans find them washed up on the beach and put them back in the sea, and often the mermaid rewards them with some treasure they find under a rock. The mother

of the Breton hero Rannou saved a mermaid, who gave her a conch shell for her son; filled with a magic potion, it endowed him with strength and power which surpassed all other men.
Popular folktales relate these marvellous legends: A mermaid was in the habit of coming each day to untangle the fair locks of the King of Romania, who had fallen into the water. Another took home to her watery palace a young girl thrown into the sea by her wicked nanny, and

gave her a magic ointment which she used to revive her drowned brother.

Tritons

The nereid Amphitritus married the sea god Poseidon and bore him a son, Triton, a sea god with the torso of a man and the tail of a fish. He lived in a gilded palace on the sea bed, and owned a conch shell with a sound so pure that it could be heard oceans away.
Triton gave birth to all the tritons, a type of merman with a bearded face and a fish's tail. In the second century, Pausanias described them as having seaweed hair, a body covered with tough little scales, gills behind their ears, a plain nose and a large, toothless slit for a mouth; they had twin shells for hands, and their legs were sometimes joined

or else separated, but always in the form of a fishtail. Riding astride dolphins, and armed with their conches, they are the roaring sounds of the sea personified. When Julius Caesar was preparing to cross the Rubicon, a triton rose up out of the reeds and blew into his conch shell to encourage the emperor. The tritons were also reputed for their extreme and lascivious lifestyle.

FRESHWATER CREATURES

Naiads

Painting (left): Water nymphs, *1927, Gaston Bussiere (1862–1929), oil on canvas, private collection, with permission of Julian Hartnoll,* © Giraudon/Bridgeman Art Library

Naiads or water-sprites are aquatic nymphs found in rivers, streams, springs and fountains. In Greek mythology, they are the daughters of Zeus and mothers of satyrs and silenes. Hermes and Dionysus were raised by the naiads.

They have the appearance of ravishingly beautiful young women with garlands of flowers in their hair. They attract the attention of handsome young men, who lose their reason at the mere sight of them, and immediately dive into the sea after them. A legend from the Pyrenees relates how "a young lord, seduced by the fairy from a spring close to Carouge, followed her into the water, and after one night of love, she allowed him to return to his castle."[77]

But in most cases, the naiads' lovers never return, and remain underwater prisoners for ever. This is the reason why, in olden times, people were warned never to go too close to springs and fountains, for fear of falling under the spell of these adorable

77. Karl des Monts, *Légendes des Pyrénées,* Paris, [no date].

but dangerous young women. Ismaël Mérindol tells how, whenever he wished to drink from a spring, he always closed his eyes before bending over the water, to avoid the risk of succumbing to the seductive smile of a naiad: "Better to drink fresh spring water without seeing it, than to drown in it with your eyes wide open," he would say.[78]

THE LADIES OF THE FOUNTAINS

naiads are responsible for the upkeep of fountains, for mostly it was they who created them, either by stamping on the ground with their foot, or in crying over a lost love. For this reason, many fountains are named after

them, with names such as: the fairy fountain, or the ladies' fountain.

These ladies attend to their toilet in the pure spring waters and comb their long tresses while sitting on a stone nearby. They dislike being watched or disturbed. "Around Condé, the villagers would keep well away from the Ladies' Fountain at night. A peasant happened to be passing by and saw a young girl dressed in white sitting on a mossy stone. She was grooming her tangled golden locks and didn't seem to notice him. The peasant stopped in surprise, but since he could not turn back, he continued on his way. As he drew near her he said: 'Mademoiselle, you are early with your toilet this evening.' The young girl cast him a cold, disdainful look and replied: 'Be gone, monsieur! While the day is yours, the night is mine'; and she went on combing her beautiful hair."[79]

Naiads will not hesitate to drown mortals who are too curious and who lean over fountains to look more closely at their underwater kingdom. If humans show disrespect, they dry up springs and stem the flow of fountains. Above all, they detest dirty people who pollute the water they use for washing. If this happens, they seek cruel revenge on the culprits, then leave the place for ever. However, they appreciate people leaving them small offerings which are of little value to humans, but priceless to them. They especially love broken plates and

78. Ismaël Mérindol, *Traité de Faërie*, 1466.
79. Paul Sébillot, *Croyances, mythes et légendes des pays de France, Les Eaux douces*, (1904–1906), Omnibus, 2002.

bottles, bread crusts and hairpins. The Abbott Piederrière (1810–1886) tells how these little gifts used to please the naiad hidden in the famous Barenton fountain, in the forest of Broceliande: "We always made sure we took with us some bread and some hairpins. Whenever we threw them into the water, the fairy would laugh with glee, and bubbles would rise up out of the silt and come to the surface like crystal pearls."[80]

SLAVIC NAIADS

The Norwegian *fossegrim* is a beautiful blonde-haired naiad standing less than thirty centimetres tall. They hide behind waterfalls and sing sweetly to the nostalgic sounds of their violins, which makes the trees quiver and stops the cascading water. The Swedish *strömkarl* play their violins by mills and falls, while in Russia, *roussalki* comb their hair and sing in the rivers and in the Black Sea. Whenever a young girl drowns, she becomes a *roussalki*, with pale skin and greenish eyes and a robe of mist. For protection against their fatal charms, people carry an absinthe leaf. In the Netherlands, *merminnes* have herring-

bone teeth and sea-green hair. The Russian *vodianoi* are actually naiads with green hair and bloated bodies like drowned corpses. They swim near water mills and anyone who catches sight of them is struck down with dropsy. Many other water creatures are found in Germanic and Nordic folk legends: *wassernixen, wellenmädchen, wasserholde, brunnenholde, wasserfrauen, seejungfrauen*, and *meerweiber*, along with thousands of others.

Nymphs

Nymphs, whose name means "fertile women", are minor goddesses in antiquity who personify the vital forces of nature. They watch over thermal springs in particular. Because of their caring nature they make excellent nannies – the god Zeus was raised by the nymph Melissa. They also protect young and betrothed girls, encourage good health and can foretell the future. Because of their feminine appearance, they are identified with sensuality, even to the point of eroticism, to which we owe the term "nymphomania". They are often depicted semi-clothed or naked, holding in their hands a seashell or an urn from which they pour water from their spring. "The nymph hour" is the fifth hour of daylight (eleven o'clock in the morning), and traditionally the time for bathing.

Oft times have I bathed
Just as the nymph hour
[chimed.[81]

NYMPHS, NYMPHOMANIACS

This aspect of their love life and fertility ensures the continuation of their race and the immortality of their souls. Paracelsus explains: "To more clearly prove their existence, God allows nymphs to be seen by some men, and even to have relations with them which produce children. These children are born into

80. Cited by Félix Bellamy, *La Forêt de Bréchéliant*, Rennes, 1896.
81. Ismaël Mérindol, *Traité de Faërie*, 1466.

the human race and have souls. A female nymph who receives this soul along with the seed will be saved by Christ. That is why nymphs seek out our love. If the nymph dies, this union cannot be dissolved, for she holds the man's soul, and should he wish to take another wife, she will return to kill him."[82]

Paracelsus illustrated this indissolubility of the marriages between humans and nymphs with the famous tale of the nymph of Stauffenberg, recounted by the Abbot of Villars: "Genies are cruel and jealous creatures, and the divine Paracelsus tells of an incident which was witnessed by all the townsfolk of Stauffenberg. "A philosopher had an eternal relationship with a nymph and thus had enjoyed the most precious of gifts from her, but was dishonest enough to love a woman as well. While dining with his new

82. Paracelsus, *A Book
on Nymphs, Sylphs,
Pygmies and
Salamanders and on the
Other Spirits*, 1566.

83. Abbé Montfaucon
de Villars, *Le Comte de
Gabalis*, Paris, 1670.

84. Karl Grün, *Les
Esprits élémentaires*,
Verviers, 1891.

mistress and a few friends, there appeared in the air before them the most delectable thigh in the world. The invisible lover wished to draw the attention of the party to his infidelity, and the stupidity of his preference for a woman. After which the indignant nymph caused him to die within the hour."[83]

NYMPHS IN GREEK ANTIQUITY

According to Karl Grün: "There is water everywhere. The number of nymphs must have been considerable, not only in oceans, lakes, rivers and springs, but also in meadows and woods where the

soil is damp, wherever streams flow and where mountains reach the clouds. Water is even to be found in the air, in the form of steam and cloud."[84] In Greek antiquity, ephidryads (water nymphs) were classified as oceanids and nereids (marine nymphs), naiads, crinaea and pegaea (spring and fountain nymphs), potamides (river nymphs) and limoniads (meadow nymphs). There are also uranies (celestial nymphs), epigeans (terrestrial nymphs), oreads (mountain nymphs), napaea and auloniads (valley nymphs), meliae (tree nymphs), dryads and hamadryads (forest nymphs) and corycids (cave nymphs). Nymphs were not immortal, but they lived for very long periods. Plutarch estimated they had a lifespan of 9,620 years. Hesiodus believed that hamadryads could live for up to 933,120 years. Endowed with the gifts of clairvoyancy and secret sciences, nymphs could inspire any mortal they chose. Cassotis assisted the priestesses of Apollo at Delphi, by inspiring their oracles. This power was later to be outlawed by the Church, which considered nymphs to be on the same level as demons: "The proof that they are indeed demons is that the Greeks said that a person was 'filled with nymphs', meaning that they were possessed by demons."[85]

Ondins and ondines

The name "ondin" comes from "onde" meaning wave. These are freshwater creatures who live in lakes, rivers or waterfalls. They are commonly found in Germanic and Scandinavian mythology. They also have lesser-known, more discreet female companions called "ondines". Unlike mermaids, ondines have bodies exactly like women, without scales on the lower half. Paracelsus wrote: "They appear in human form, dressed like us. They are extremely beautiful and eager to tempt us with their crafty wiles."[86]
Ondines attract and seduce young men, then lead them into the waves, and down

While bathing, the ondines comb their long golden tresses

to their magnificent crystal palaces, from whence they rarely return.
Karl Grün paints the following portrait: "Ondines are always pretty, malicious and sometimes cruel. They come to the surface to groom their hair, which consists of blonde or aqua-coloured seaweed. They turn their smiling faces to passers-by, to reveal their shining coral lips and sparkling green eyes. Any young man who sees them instantly falls under the spell of such beauty. He follows the ondine to her underwater crystal palace to live with her there. But in this watery environment, days pass like minutes. The man is not aware of this, and when he returns to land, he is surprised to meet the great-

85. Collin de Plancy, *Dictionnaire infernal*, 1825–1826.
86. Paracelsus, *A Book on Nymphs, Sylphs, Pygmies and Salamanders and on the Other Spirits*, 1566.

Lorelei!

Lorelei!

Lorelei!

grandchildren of people he previously knew! Everyone mocks him, for he is wearing ridiculous clothes which went out of date long ago."[87]

Ondine by Frédéric de la Motte-Fouqué (1811) is an adaptation of an ancient German legend, which tells the story of a water fairy who falls in love with a mortal, thereby ensuring that his soul will become immortal. From being a simple creature in an unconscious state, she passes to a conscious state in which she becomes aware of human emotions and suffering, which finally results in her death. Hans Christian Andersen explores this theme in his tale of the *Little Mermaid*.

Once married to a human, an ondine can never return to the water without risking death: "Even now people still say that whoever has an ondine for his wife must avoid taking her on the water, and above all, avoid

upsetting her if she finds herself in water. If these rules are not respected the ondine will return for ever to the sea, without dissolving the marriage. If the abandoned husband remarries, the ondine will kill him."[88]

This indissolubility of marriage with ondines also applied to nymphs.

LORELEI AND THE DAUGHTERS OF THE RHINE

The Rhine was the home of some famous ondines, including Lorelei, the beautiful ondine of Bacharach-on-Rhine, who sat on a rock near the river bank combing her long golden locks and contemplating her face reflected in the water, as she sang a nostalgic song with the chorus: *Lorelei! Lorelei! Lorelei!*

Gérard de Nerval tells the tale: "You and I both know her, my friend, as Lorely or Lorelei, the fairy of the Rhine, whose tiny pink toes fly surely over the slippery rocks of Bacharach, near Coblenz. You have seen her graceful long neck and her lithe body. Her garnet-red hood, the brim trimmed with gold, shines from afar like the bloodied crest of the ancient dragon of Eden.

"Her long yellow tresses tumble down over her white shoulders like a golden torrent cascading into the deep green waters of the river. Her bended knee peeks out from beneath the green brocaded robe clinging about her thighs.

"Her left arm is draped lightly around the mandore of the old Minnesängers of Thuringer, and between those beguiling rose-studded breasts, her pleated tunic is loosely tied with a spangled ribbon. She smiles with an invincible grace, and from her parted lips flow the songs of the sirens of antiquity."[89]

This emblematic figure of the Rhine also inspired many poets and musicians, including Heinrich Heine:

In vain would I seek to discover
Why sad and mournful am I;
My thoughts without ceasing brood over
A tale of the times gone by.

The air is cool, and it darkleth,
And calmly flows the Rhine;
The peak of the mountain sparkleth,
While evening's sun doth shine.

Yon sits a wondrous maiden
On high, a maiden fair;
With bright gleaming jewels all-laden,
She combs her golden hair.

She tends it with comb all-golden,
And sings the while a song;
How strange is that melody olden,
As gently it echoes along!

It fills with wild terror the sailor
At sea in his tiny skiff;
He looks but on high, and grows paler,
Nor sees the rock-girded cliff.

The waves will the barque and its master
At length swallow up, then methought
'Tis Lore-ley who this disaster
With her false singing hath wrought.

In *Rhinegold*, prelude to Richard Wagner's *Tetralogy*, inspired by the Germanic legend of the Niebelungen, the daughters of the Rhine, Woglinde, Welgunde and Flosshilde, are ondines responsible for guarding the treasures hidden in the river. The dwarf Alberich steals this fabulous wealth from them, and forges a ring of gold with the power to start wars and inflame jealousy until the end of time.

STAGNANT WATERS AND MARSHES

Night Washerwomen

Laundresses of death, women of the night, singers of the night; lavandières de nuit, lessiveuses de la mort (France); pâles de nuit (in the Franche-Comté region); bugadiero (Provence)

These supernatural washerwomen appear at night around stagnant waters or riverside washing places, and make their presence felt with the sounds of their singing and the flailing of wet linen. To

89. Gérard de Nerval, *Souvenirs d'Allemagne.*

Night washerwomen, night laundresses, laundresses of death, women of the night, singers of the night, pale night women, bugadiera

meet them means bad luck, and sometimes even imminent death.

Unlike the water fairies, who also come to the river banks to do their washing, and get their linen "fairy white", or like the mermaids, who launder their linen in the foaming sea, or the *incantados,* those half-angel, half-serpent creatures who plunge their laundry into sacred springs, the night washerwomen are creatures with morbid instincts who must be avoided at all costs. Usually they are witches, or dead souls who have not been wrapped in a clean funeral shroud, and who come back at night to wash it; or else they are ghosts come back to earth to atone for their sins.

Most commonly they committed transgressions in life, such as daring to do their

90. Ismaël Mérindol,
Traité de Faërie, 1466.

laundry on a Sunday rather than respecting the Sabbath rest day, being too economical with their soap, or having killed their own offspring: in this case they are condemned to eternally launder the bloodied linen

of their lifeless babes. In Lower Brittany, the swaddling clothes they hold out to passersby contain the crushed body of an infant, and at Dinant, the night washerwomen scrub the bones of infants who died unbaptised.

In Provence, the *bugadiero* are witches or "masks", who invite young men to come dance with them, then seize the opportunity to push them into the water, where they proceed to devour them. Many times when he was a child, the Provençal Ismaël Mérindol, encountered the emaciated forms of these monstrous washerwomen. Already familiar with various remedies against spells, he made them flee with this rhyme:

Begone Bugadiero,
Masco begone!
Here's my foot in your
[behind! [90]

In Brittany they are known as *ar kan-nerez-noz,* "singers of the night". They appear on the odd hours during the night and with their fine white hair they weave sheets and shrouds, which they then launder in the river. Collin de Plancy considers these spiteful monsters to be a type of White Lady: "White Ladies who do their washing while singing in the moonlight by far-off springs are known as 'night washerwomen or singers of the night'. Should someone pass by around midnight, they ask for help with wringing out their laundry. But if he dares grumble, they twist it so hard and so fast that the arms of their unfortunate victim are soon broken."[91]

At the Oberbronn washhouse in Alsace, a White Lady set herself apart from the other washerwomen, and silently scrubbed the shirts of the dead. Cambry also reports that these night washerwomen "invite you to wring their sheets, break your arms if you complain, and drown you if you refuse them".[92] The following tale, told by Émile Souvestre and reported by Paul Sébillot, illustrates the cruelty of these night washer-women: "A young man from Léon had spent All Saints eve carousing instead of praying for the dead. As he neared a stream he saw the *kannerez-noz* at the *douez*, or washing place, beating their linen and singing their sad refrains; they ran to him with their funeral shrouds, asking him for help to wring them out. He agreed,

and to avoid being crushed, he first twisted in the same direction as they did; but the other washerwomen, some of whom he recognised as his dead relatives, reproached him for letting them miss prayers. Troubled by these accusations, he twisted in the wrong direction; instantly his hands were crushed and he dropped dead, a victim of the washer-women."[93] It is also said that "instead of being twisted tight, as usual, the linen swells, and instead of wringing out water, you can see the shape of a body in it. The fairy twists faster, drawing you to her, then she casts a fold of the shroud over your shoulder and winds you into it".[94]

In his work *The Last Fairies,* Paul Féval quotes the following refrain, sung by the night washerwomen:
Wring out the rags,
Wring out the shrouds,
For the widows of the dead.
In the Berry region, the night washerwomen launder "a kind of blood-red vaporous veil with a transparency like opal. It seems to take on a human form and people swear that it weeps. Some say washerwomen are the souls of unbaptised dead infants or adults who have not received the sacrament of confirmation; they carry out their work relentlessly, and

Illustration above:
© *Sandrine Gestin*

almost always in silence".[95] But making the sign of the cross is all it takes to make these damned souls disappear.

Nixes and nixies

Neckers (Hollande)

In Germanic and Nordic legends, male nixes are old men with a long beard, horrible green teeth and a green hat. They are usually treacherous creatures who love dancing and music. In Germany, whenever a man drowns, they say: "The nixes have taken him away",

91. Collin de Plancy, *Dictionnaire infernal,* 1825–1826.
92. Cambry, *Voyage dans le Finistère,* Brest, 1836.
93. Émile Souvestre, *Le Foyer breton,* Paris, 1852, and Paul Sébillot, *Croyances, mythes et légendes des pays de France, Les Eaux douces,* (1904–1906), Omnibus, 2002.
94. N. Quellien, *Contes et Nouvelles du pays de Tréguier,* Paris, 1899.
95. Paul Sébillot, *Légendes et Curiosités des métiers,* Flammarion, [no date].

and Luther mentions them in his writings.

Their companions are the ravishingly beautiful nixies, feminine creatures with graceful features and long blonde hair, who usually live in stagnant backwaters. Nixies are often cruel, and spend their days trying to attract young men to their watery lairs, and drowning them.

DANCE OF THE NIXIES

Sometimes, they will even attend balls, dressed as vivacious and elegant young women, who seduce their dancing partners, taking them off to their deadly fate at the bottom of some nearby pond. In Holland they are known as *neckers*, and they join in the dancing with the locals, causing young girls to drown in the murky waters. The dance of the nixies is always a precursor to the death of whoever joins in.

"Whoever dances with a nixie immediately notices that her frock is made of a delicate fabric, and that her bearing is mysterious and aristocratic. They have a sensitive and poetic nature, but at the same time they are very noble and proud."[96]

whoever crosses their path.

In the quivering reeds around the islets and marshes of the Rhone river, near Lake Léman, live the *fenettes*, or "little ladies": "These lithe, fine-featured fairies with

green eyes and long hair do not often show themselves. But whenever their voices are heard more clearly nearby, the fisherman winds in his line, the reaper lays down his scythe, the hunter retreats and all take care not to look back, for fear of seeing the *fenette* coming after him:

Water witches

Blanquettes (Gascogne), fenettes (Alps of the Vaud region), macrales d'aïe (Liege), marluzennes (Hainaut), martes (Berry), groac'h (Brittany)

Water witches haunt marshes or river banks. To meet one spells danger: they devour or announce death to

Blanquettes,
fenettes,
macrales
d'aïe,
marluzennes,
martes,
groac'h

Illustrations:
© Sandrine Gestin

96. Karl Grün, *Les Esprits élémentaires,* Verviers, 1891.

Illustration:
© Sandrine Gestin

The wivre may be recognised by the garnet carbuncle she wears on her forehead

97. A. Ceresole,
*Légendes des Alpes
vaudoises*, Lausanne,
1885.
98. Jean d'Arras, *Le
Roman de Mélusine*,
1387.

*Illustration: ©
Sandrine Gestin*

he who has seen one of these little fairies in the wild will be sure to die by the year's end."[97] In the Berry district, the *martes* can be seen beside waterfalls, sometimes as fairies, but more often in the form of witches. In her work *Rustic Legends*, George Sand mentions the sounds of their wailing and cursing.

In the south of Brittany, *groac'h* are water witches who live underwater in ponds or lakes. Pierre Souvestre refers to the *groac'h* of the island of Lok, who owned treasures of inestimable value. Whoever tried to steal them was turned into a fish, until the day a foolhardy youth put an end to the *groac'h*'s spell using Saint Corentin's knife. But when he tried to escape, the witch caught him and changed him into a frog.

Wivres

Vouivre, wivre, wouivre, wouavre, guivre

Wivres adopt two forms: sometimes they appear as a splendid naiad, and may be recognised by the gemstone carbuncle on their forehead, or sometimes in the form of a dragon or a winged serpent. When swimming, they remove their precious carbuncle and hide it safely in the grass, or in a crevice in the rocks before diving into the water. Any mortal who steals this incomparable jewel without being caught by the wivre is sure to become rich and powerful.

Every Saturday, Mélusine, the fairy of Poitou, saw the lower half of her body transformed into a snake's tail, and one day she was unexpectedly caught in that guise by her husband, come to spy on her in her bath; at this she changed herself into a winged serpent. For this reason, she should be considered as much a wivre as a fairy or a White Lady.[98]

The earth people

The earth people: ARRAGOUSSETS • BERGLEUTES • DUERGARS
ERDLUITLES • GNOMES • GOBLINS • KNOCKERS • KOBOLDS
LAMINAKS • DWARVES • NIBELUNG • PYGMIES • Stone and
ruin dwellers: RED CAPS • KORRIGANS

-4-

*T*he earth people, dwarves, gnomes and
other korrigans, live deep underground, in dark caves
and in ruins, amongst piles of rubble. Do not judge
them by their size. Skilled metalsmiths, and experts
in magic, these hardworking people wield great
power, for they are the guardians of many a secret
and hidden treasures. These ugly, misshapen little
monsters are liars, cheats and thieves; for the earth
people are usually ill-disposed towards humans, and
it is never wise to show a lack of respect for them. But
the rare chosen ones they do like will never have
reason to criticise their generosity or their gold …

THE EARTH PEOPLE

Arragoussets

Sarregousets

These troglodytic dwarves from the Anglo-Norman isles, and particularly Guernsey, originally came from a cave on the west coast known as the *Creux des Fées*, or The Fairy Hollow, and later they invaded and destroyed the whole of the island. Paul Sébillot writes: "A man named Jean Letocq rose one morning earlier than usual to go to his sheepfold. There he saw large numbers of wee folk coming out of the Fairy Hollow armed with all sorts of weapons; despite the resistance put up by the townspeople, they quickly took over the whole island, killing the men and taking possession of their women and their homes. Two inhabitants escaped this carnage: a man and a young boy from the parish of Saint-André, who managed to hide inside a large oven. For many years the invaders, who

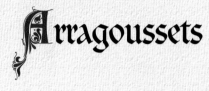

*Illustration:
Cave near St Agnes,
Thomas Jones
(1743–1803), oil on
paper, National Museum
and Gallery of Wales,
Cardiff, ©
Giraudon/Bridgeman
Art Library*

Illustration:
Snow White, *Roland
Risse (1835–?), Christie's
Images, London,
© Giraudon/Bridgeman
Art Library*

*The dwarves
in Snow
White belong
to the
Bergleute tribe*

belonged to the fairy race, lived peacefully with the women they had taken captive, and acted like good family men, raising more sons and daughters. The short stature and the superior intelligence of certain families on the island is said to be due to this intermarriage of the two races." [99]

In *The Workers of the Sea* Victor Hugo refers to them as *sarregousets*: "At night when it thunders, if you should happen to see men flying amongst the fiery clouds or on the rolling waves of air, they are none other than the *sarregousets*. One woman who lives at Grand-Mielles knew them well. One evening there were some *sarregousets* at a cross-road, where a man driving a cart had stopped to find his way. The woman called to him: 'Ask them the way, they're always ready to help a stranger, the ones to give you advice.' There can be little doubt that this woman was a sorceress."

For some unknown reason, one day the arragoussets left their wives, children and homes to live invisibly. But sometimes they return at night to visit their former homes and carry out small housekeeping tasks.

Bergmännchen

99. Paul Sébillot,
*Croyances, mythes et
légendes des pays de
France, La Mer,*
(1904–1906), Omnibus,
2002.

Bergleutes

Bergmännchen

Beugleutes or "mountain people", a race of dwarf miners living in Germany, and the *bergmännchen* or "little mountain people", are happy, industrious, peaceful and generous. They take great care to protect injured animals and children lost in the forest. Like the dwarves in *Snow White*, they live in pretty thatched cottages in the forest, close to the mine where they work. While their history is hard to determine, they were reported as working in diamond mines during the sixteenth century.

The bergleutes have such an affinity with the minerals they extract from the earth that they are capable of feeling their emotions. For them, copper, quartz or schist are much more than simple minerals; they have real emotions which the dwarves can understand. One dwarf, named Nickel, was so attached to this metal that he named it after himself.

While they are usually good natured and helpful, bergleutes may sometimes play nasty tricks on miners. The writer Frédéric Piton relates how in the mid-nineteenth century, an old miner from Alsace told him how the bergleutes would tease him by throwing handfuls of dirt in his face, blowing out his lamp or hiding his tools. Fortunately this type of nasty behaviour appears to be quite exceptional.

Duergars

Dvergars, black dwarves

Duergars are dwarf miners and blacksmiths who live in the Nordic countries and in the north of England. For Sir Walter Scott, "They were a little, diminutive race, but possessed of some skill probably in mining or smelting minerals, with which the country abounds. Perhaps also they might, from their acquaintance with the changes of the clouds, or meteorological phenomena, be judges of weather, and so enjoy another title to supernatural skill."[100] They only reach knee height, compared with normal men, but they are stocky and strong. They wear sheepskin jackets, moleskin trousers and shoes, and a hat of moss-green trimmed with a pheasant's feather. Duergars have dark, nasty temperaments. If by chance they meet a man lost in the dark, they glare at him with obvious hostility and go out of their way to play nasty tricks on him.

Yet during the eighteenth century, the Lutheran pastor Einard Gudmund considered them as "creatures of God with a body and a soul, capable of reasoning, subject to death, and constantly trying to establish romantic relations with humans and acquire the benefits of baptism." But most observers dispute this optimistic view. Grice relates the following tale:

Dwarves shun the sunlight, which instantly turns them to stone

*Illustration:
© Sandrine Gestin*

100. Sir Walter Scott, *Histoire de la démonologie et de la sorcellerie*, translation by M. Defauconpret, Furne Éditeur, Paris, 1832.

Erdluitles

Bergmanli, härdmandlene, heidenmanndli, gotwergi (Germany), guriuz (Italy). Female forms: erdbibberli, erdweibchen, hei-denweibchen, herdweibche

"A stranger lost in the hills of Northumberland had lit a fire for the night when a fearsome-looking duergar stomped over and sat down on a stone beside him, took an enormous log and snapped it across his knee as though it were matchwood. Then he threw the pieces away with a defiant air. Not wanting to upset the duergar, the traveller dared not retrieve the wood for the dying fire. But by daybreak, the duergar had gone, and the lone traveller was astonished to see that the pieces of wood lay perched at the edge of a deep ravine, down which he would certainly have tumbled to his death."[101]

The Brown Man of the Muirs was a duergar from the Scottish border country, a guardian of wild animals, who was nevertheless most hostile towards humans.

The erdluitles, who live mostly in Germany, but also in the north of Italy, are a very old race of mountain-dwelling dwarves. Their name means "people of the earth". They are no taller than a seven-year-old, their skin is the colour of the earth, and their hair is dark and curly. They have animal-shaped ears and webbed feet of which they are sorely ashamed, and which they try but fail to hide beneath their clothing of red and black hoods and long green or blue-grey overshirts. They feed mainly on roots, berries and peas, but they also enjoy grilled pig meat. Their tempestuous natures enable them to cause storms, tempests and avalanches. But they also assist with the germination of plants by performing magic dances, and advise peasants of the best times to plant seed. What is more, they can transform ordinary leaves into diamonds or gold. Erdluitles take care of flocks and herds of

animals, especially chamois goats. They are famed for their chamois milk cheese, and keep the recipe tightly guarded. Their womenfolk, the *'erdbibberlis'* or *'erdweibchens'*, are excellent weavers who find work on local farms.

Playful, noisy and boisterous creatures who enjoy carousing, the erdluitles organise wedding feasts in isolated barns and lofts. In exchange for the friendly welcome they receive from humans, they shower them with gifts and playthings; these are usually a few lumps of

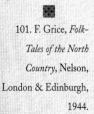

101. F. Grice, *Folk-Tales of the North Country*, Nelson, London & Edinburgh, 1944.

coal, which change into a precious jewel come morning.

STILLE VOLK AND QUIET FOLK

The stille volk and quiet folk are closely related to the erdluitles, although they are infinitely more peaceful. These malformed, lame people have dark skin and wiry grey hair, with unusually dense beards and eyebrows. Like their cousins, they also have webbed feet which they hide beneath their rough grey clothing, and their red or grey hoods endow them with extraordinary strength and the power to become invisible.

The stille volk are thousands of years old; they know all the secrets of the earth, its minerals and precious stones, and use these for their remedies, with the result that they are never ill. They are skilful blacksmiths, and despite being immensely rich, they also know how to spin, weave, bake bread

and brew beer.

Like most dwarves, above all, the stille volk fear the sound of bells and sunlight, and so they make their homes in dark caves, in burrows under hills, and also in barns.[102]

Gnomes

Gnomes are a race of very wise underground dwarves. The most widely accepted etymology of the word "gnome" is that it stems from the low Latin *gnomus* and from the Greek *gnosis*, meaning "knowledge". *The Oxford English Dictionary* suggests an elision of *genomus*, "earth

dwelling". Huygin and Poortvliet[103] report that in 1200 AD the Swede Frederik Ugarp discovered in a fisherman's cabin a fifteen-centimetre high wood-and-poly chrome statuette with the words "GNOME, full size" on the base. This statuette belongs to the private collection of the Oliv family in Uppsala. The same authors cite the eyewitness account of a retired sergeant from the Roman troops, Publius Octavus, living near Leyden in the Netherlands, who noted in his diary in 470: "Today I saw with my own eyes a miniature man. He was wearing a red cap and a blue shirt. He had a white beard and green trousers. He told me he had lived in our area for only about twenty years. He spoke our language, mixed with foreign words. I have since spoken with him on several occasions. He told me he comes from the Kuwald race, a word I am not familiar with, and he added that there are not many in these parts. His favourite drink is milk. Many times I have seen him cure ailing cattle in two days."[104]

In his *Traité de Faërie*, published in 1466, Ismaël Mérindol refers to an old

Les nains redoutent la lumière du soleil, qui les pétrifie instantanément

102. Cited by Nancy Arrowsmith and George Moorse, *A Field Guide to the Little People*, Pocket Books, New York, 1977.
103. Will Huygen and Rien Poortvliet, *Les Gnomes*, Albin Michel, 1979.
104. Will Huygen and Rien Poortvliet, *Les Gnomes*, Albin Michel, 1979.

gnome he met in Prague who was nearing the end of his life on Earth, and who passed on to him a body of knowledge, a small part of which the writer reproduced. This famous work has remained largely unread, as the only extant copy is housed in the closed stacks of the Prague National Library. Many notable scientists, writers and artists sought inspiration from this source material and, in particular, Leonardo da Vinci, who cites Mérindol in his notes. In a work entitled *De Hominibus Parvissimis* (The Smallest Men), written in 1580, Wilhelm J. Wunderlich tells how at that time there still existed gnomes who had lived for over a thousand years in an egalitarian society without rich or poor, and which was governed by a king elected from the gnome community.

THE EARTH, NATURAL ENVIRONMENT OF GNOMES

The cabalists believed that gnomes were simple spirits composed of the finest parts of the earth in which they lived. Paracelsus gives an account in

his work on the elemental creatures: "Such is the case of the mountain gnomes; the earth is their air and their vital element: for everything lives in its vital element; this means that living things live, walk and stand up in it. So the earth is nothing more than the vital element of the mountain dwarves: since, like spirits, they

pass through walls, rock and stone, leaving them intact (…) this amounts to saying that mountains, earth and rocks hamper them no more in their activities than the air hampers us in ours. To move about while surrounded by air without it being any obstacle to us is an equally insignificant thing as rocks and cliffs are for them."[105] Collin de Plancy reports that the Earth "is filled almost to

the centre with gnomes, small people, guardians of treasures, of mines and quarries. They like humans, are clever and easily managed. They supply the cabalists with all the money they need, and in return for their services, all they ask is to receive orders from their masters. Their womenfolk, the gnomides, are tiny but pleasant, although they dress in a rather curious manner. Gnomes live and die in a similar way to humans; they have cities and their communities are well organised. The cabalists claim that the noises heard, and reported by Aristotle as coming from certain islands, even where no inhabitants were to be seen, were nothing more than the merrymaking and wedding festivities of some gnome. They have a mortal soul; but by contracting marriage with

105. Paracelsus, *Nymphs, Sylphs, Pygmies and Salamanders and on the Other Spirits, 1566.*

humans, they can achieve immortality."[106]

Karl Grün writes: "In Judaic cabalistics, the gnomes know the secrets of the earth; they animate plants and animals, and once they leave, the living thing dies. (…) Originally, gnomes only had one foot. Their women, called 'gnomides', are much smaller, exquisitely pretty, superbly dressed, and walk lightly in silent slippers, one studded with emeralds and the other with rubies. Not only are gnomes tiny, they are infinitely small, for they can pass through fissures in the earth, deep within crystalline caves where green stalactites hang from above. They slumber gently beneath vaulted arches of gold and silver. The gnomides are responsible for guarding precious gemstones."[107]

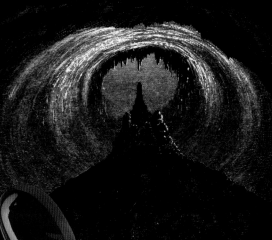

GUARDIANS OF TREASURE

Gnomes are the guardians of treasure buried deep in the bowels of the earth, as Paracelsus relates: "God has set in place guardians to watch over everything in nature, and never to leave anything unguarded. So it is that the gnomes, pygmies and manes – departed spirits of the dead – guard the earth's metals and other similar treasures. For where they dwell may be found enormous quantities of treasure of inestimable value, and these creatures look after them, secreted and hidden away from our eyes, only to be revealed at the proper time. When they are finally discovered, people say: 'In olden times mountain dwarves and gnomes lived here, but now, times have changed', meaning that the time has come to reveal these riches. For the earth's wealth is distributed in such a way that, since the beginning of time, metals such as silver, gold and iron have been discovered not all at once, but rather, one by one, and these creatures make sure that they are found little by little, now in one country, then in another. Thus, mines move about in time and space, and chronologically they will continue to exist from the first to the very last day."[108]

Gnomes are also responsible for the germination of plants and the care of tree roots. According to certain writings of the Talmud and the Hebraic Cabala, a gnome assisted with the edification of the Temple of Solomon.

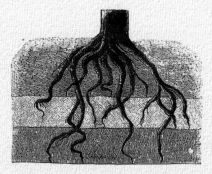

GNOMES AND DEMONS IN HELL

For the Abbé Montfaucon de Villars, the underground proximity of the gnomes to demons in hell sometimes causes them to renounce their long-standing alliance

Gnomes are the guardians of the earth's treasures

106. Collin de Plancy, *Dictionnaire infernal*, 1825–1826.

107. Karl Grün, *Les Esprits élémentaires*, Verviers, 1891.

108. Paracelsus, *A Book on Nymphs, Sylphs, Pygmies and Salamanders and on the Other Spirits*, 1566.

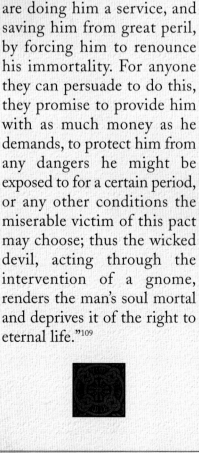

with man and to reject the immortality of the human soul. Thus they become accomplices of the devil: "These gnomes, frightened by the howlings of the devils, which they hear in the centre of the earth, choose to remain mortal, rather than run the risk of being so tormented had they acquired immortality. For this reason, the gnomes and their neighbours the devils have some correspondence with each other. The latter persuade the gnomes, who are naturally great friends to man, that they are doing him a service, and saving him from great peril, by forcing him to renounce his immortality. For anyone they can persuade to do this, they promise to provide him with as much money as he demands, to protect him from any dangers he might be exposed to for a certain period, or any other conditions the miserable victim of this pact may choose; thus the wicked devil, acting through the intervention of a gnome, renders the man's soul mortal and deprives it of the right to eternal life."[109]

Goblins

Bogies, bogles, fanfrelons

Goblins which must not be confused with hob-goblins, are imps who are friendly towards humans, and live in English homes alongside their human residents; however, they are grotesquely ugly, and almost always wicked troublemakers. Most goblins are miners. In his writings entitled *De Animantis Subterranibus* (Basel, 1651), Georgius Agricola refers to "the

Illustration: The Temptation of Saint Anthony, David Teniers (the Younger) (1610–1690), oil on canvas, private collection, Johnny Van Haeften Ltd., London, © Giraudon/Bridgeman Art Library

Bogies, bogles, fanfrelons

109. Abbé Montfaucon de Villars, *Le Comte de Gabalis*, Paris, 1670.

goblins who worked in the mines", and they are depicted on the title page of the book *Golden Remains of the Ever Memorable Mr John Hales* (1653). They are always shown hard at work with their picks and shovels, their hammers ringing out blows, but there is never a trace of their labour. Bogies and bogles of Scotland and England are fearsome goblins, commonly believed to be descended from the devil himself. But due to their stubborn and simple-minded nature, they are easily duped. In Wales there is a class of goblins known as fanfrelons. They are cousins of the Cornish knockers. One day, so the story goes, in the midst of a field in the parish of Bodfari, in Denbighshire, a dozen or more fanfrelons began a wild and devilish dance: "The fanfrelons were all dressed in red like English soldiers, with red and yellow polka-dotted kerchiefs knotted around their foreheads. Strangely, they were almost human-sized, but they looked so much like dwarves that they could not be called otherwise."[110]

The goblins also hold a market which is frequented only by the Little People of Fairyland. Humans who venture there, even just to browse, fall prey to these terrible sprites, who pinch them, pull their hair, and force them to eat deadly fruits.[111]

We must not look at goblin men,
We must not buy their fruits:
Who knows upon what soil
they fed
Their hungry thirsty roots?[112]

Knockers

Esprits frappeurs, petits mineurs, verts boucs, boublins (Liège), black dwarves (Scotland), coblynaus (Wales), buccas, nickers, nuggies, gathorns, spriggans (Cornwall), haussschmiedlein (Bohemia), berg-möndche, meister hämmerlinge (Germany), schacht-zwergen (Austria)

Knockers are dwarves which are found commonly in the mines of Scotland, where they are nicknamed "black dwarves", but also in Cornwall, where they haunt the tin mines, in Wales, where they are found in the coal mines, and in the silver mines of Bohemia.

In Germany they are called "monks of the mountains" or "master hammer-smiths", and in Austria, "extraction dwarves". Around Liege, and in Rumania and the former Yugoslavia, miners consider them as bad omens. According to Katharine Briggs, they are the ghosts of Jews who worked in the mines

Illustration:
© Sandrine Gestin

110. Wirt Sikes, *English Goblins*, Sampson Low, Marston, Searle and Rivington, 1880, cited by Brian Froud and Alan Lee, *Les Fées*, Albin Michel, 1978.
111 and 112. Christina Rossetti, *Goblin Market*, 1862.

Knockers, little
miners, green
billygoats, verts
oucs, fanfrelans,
boublins, black
dwarves,
coblynau, buccas,
nickers, nuggies,
gathorns,
spriggans,
nussschmiedlein,
Berg-Möndche,
Meister
Hämmerlinge,
Schacht-
Zwergen

113. Katharine Briggs,
A *Dictionary of Fairies*,
Penguin Books,
London, 1976.
114. Sir Walter Scott,
*Histoire de la
démonologie et de la
sorcellerie*, translation by
M. Defauconpret, Furne
Éditeur, Paris, 1832.

of Cornwall in the eleventh and twelfth centuries.[113] Knockers stand from forty-five to ninety centimetres high, and dress in similar clothes to the local miners. They wear large leather aprons and a studded helmet with nose and neck reinforcing, and a lighted candle on top. Once or twice a year the townsfolk leave out used children's clothing for them, for in the olden days children also worked in the mines. These clothes should always be second hand, for like most dwarves, knockers detest anything new. They delight in punishing ill-mannered people who whistle for no reason or spit, by pulling their hair or unscrewing their head, or else losing them at the bottom of the mine.

To keep on their good side, it is recommended that small offerings of food (preferably sweets) be left out for them.

Knockers adore fritters, pancakes, and waffles, and simply drool over muffins, crumpets and doughnuts.

As their name implies, knockers use their hammers and picks to chip away at the mineral-rich walls of the mineshafts, and thus attract miners. These mine dwarves know exactly where to find the best lead-, tin-, silver- or gold-bearing seams.

They also warn the mine workers of rockfalls and other dangers that await them, by hammering loudly and violently.

The Welsh coblynaus are grotesque-looking creatures dressed like miners. They always look very busy, but actually do nothing at all. They are jolly natured and pleasant to people, but throw stones at whoever makes fun of them.

Kobolds

Kobolds are spiteful German mine gnomes. In appearance and behaviour they are similar to knockers, although they are much nastier.

Sir Walter Scott described them thus: "The kobolds were a species of gnomes who haunted the dark and solitary places, and were often seen in the mines, where they seemed to imitate the labours of the miners, and sometimes took pleasure in frustrating their objects and rendering their toil unfruitful. Sometimes they were malignant, especially if neglected or insulted; but sometimes also they were indulgent to individuals whom they took under their protection. Therefore, whenever a miner hit upon a rich vein of ore, the inference commonly was, not that he possessed more skill, industry, or even luck, than his fellow workmen, but that the spirits of the mine had directed him to the treasure."[114]

Laminaks

Lamignacs, lamigna (fem.)

Laminaks are hirsute dwarves from the Basque country in the Pyrenees. While there are both males and females, the latter are relatively harmless, only coming out of their caves for ablutions and to comb their hair. But the males can very easily act violently towards human females, "and have no respect for the virtue of the peasant women whom they take prisoner in their underground caves."[115] They live among the rocks, under old bridges, deep under Mount Gastelu or on the towering summit of Isturitz. Excellents builders, in a single night they completed the Licq bridge in the Soule province, and the castles of Laustania and Donamartia in Cize. Masters of metamorphosis, in the twinkling of an eye they can change into a spider, a snake or an eel. It was they who set a trap for the knight Roland at Roncevaux.

Dwarves

Dwarves are an industrious people who live mainly in caves and underground mines. Although small, dwarves are nevertheless ten times taller than elves, and the two are quite different races. They are mentioned most often in Germanic and Nordic mythology and folklore.

According to Paracelsus: "Similarly, dwarves are the descendents of mountain-dwelling gnomes: for this reason they are not giant-sized; quite the contrary, they are even smaller than the gnomes, just as gnomes are smaller than sylphs. Just like giants, they too are monsters, and are born in the same manner."[116]

SMALL DWARVES AND LARGE DWARVES

Claude Lecouteux points out that the word "dwarf" is a generic term, like "elf" or "giant", and does not mean that dwarves are necessarily small. There are both "big" dwarves and "small" dwarves. He does concede, however, that in medieval tales "a dwarf usually measures between sixty-nine centimetres and one metre thirty-three, with small feet and short legs."[117] He adds that dwarves have "the strength of a dozen or twenty men, which certain authors attribute to the fact that they own magic objects."[118]

Usually these old, ugly and deformed dwarves are cantankerous and violent. Their name comes from the Norwegian *dvergr* and from the Old German *zwerc*, meaning "twisted", both literally and figuratively speaking.

Dwarves are excellent miners, skilful blacksmiths, talented craftsmen and inspired jewellers. They created many a legendary sword, and most of the magical objects known to us.

Lamignacs, lamigna

115. Paul Sébillot, *Croyances, mythes et légendes des pays de France, Le Monde souterrain*, (1904–1906), Omnibus, 2002.
116. Paracelsus, *A Book on Nymphs, Sylphs, Pygmies and Salamanders and on the Other Spirits, 1566.*
117 and 118. Claude Lecouteux, *Les Nains et les Elfes au Moyen Âge*, Imago, 1988.

Illustration :
© Sandrine Gestin

There are both "small" dwarves and "big" dwarves...

THE DARK DWARVES OF EDDA

In Edda, at the dawn of time, the dwarves Modsognir and Durin gave birth to a race in their own image. Four of them were entrusted by the gods to support the world, created from the quartered body of the giant Ymir.

The dwarves of Edda mingle with the *dökkalfars*, or dark elves, living in the underground darkness of Svartalfheimr and Niflheimr, as opposed to the light elves, creatures of the air, and to the ases living in the celestial kingdom of Asgard. Only Loge, the god of fire and

deception, was in the habit of leaving Asgard and venturing into the dark corridors of Niflheimr, to contrive some dastardly plot with the dwarves. As black as pitch, dwarves mainly work as blacksmiths. They are responsible for the major attributes of the ases: Thor's hammer, Odin's boar-spear, Freyr's vessel, Freya's necklace, Sif's hair, Draupnir's ring and the golden-haired boar. They also forge formidable swords which may prove fatal to humans. Experts in magic, they

are also the guardians of fabulous treasures, and the source of poetry known as "dwarves' beverage".

Voluspa, an anthology of Scandinavian legends compiled by Snorri Sturluson, the author of *Edda*, reveals the names of the underground dwarves: Nyi, Nidi, Nordri, Sudri, Austri, Vestri, Althiof, Dvalin, Nar, Nain, Niping, Dain, Bifur, Bafur, Bombor, Nori, Ori, Onar, Oin, Miodvinir, Vig, Gandalf, Vindalf, Thorin, Fili, Kili, Fundin, Vali, Thror, Throin, Thekk, Lit, Vitr, Nyr, Nyrad, Rekk and Radsvid.

The stone-dwellers are Farupnir, Dolgthvari, Haur, Hugstari, Hlediolf, Gloin, Dori, Ori, Duf, Andvari, Heptifili, Har and Sviar.

Those who live on the mudflats and the sand dunes are called Skirvir, Virvir, Skafid, Ai, Alf, Ingi, Eikinskialdi, Fal, Frosti, Fid and Ginnar.

THE KING OF THE DWARVES

Laurin is often cited as the king of the dwarves. He is three spans high, or sixty-nine centimetres, and his horse is the size of a buck. He lives in a hollow mountain in the Tyrol, where he has a magnificent rose garden. He also possesses magic weapons: a ring of power, a girdle which endows him with the strength of a dozen men, and a Tarnkappe, or mythical cloak which makes him invisible.

King Herla, sovereign of the ancient Bretons, was invited to visit a dwarf king who also lives in a hollow mountian. But on the journey home, the king realised that the three days he had spent there had actually lasted three centuries. Since that time, Herla and his knights have been condemned to wander the earth ceaselessly, without rest or respite.[119]

DWARVES' HOMES

Dwarves live in the earth "like rabbits in their burrows", writes René-François Le Men, an archivist from Finistere, who reports that they only show themselves at night, on the edges of the darkest woods, on isolated moors, or on craggy hilltops. There are also troglodyte dwarves who live in caves or crevices amongst the rocks.

A Breton rhyme reflects how dwarves remain underground during winter to escape the cold:

– Bin, ban,
Corriganan,
Pelec'h e moc'h
epad ar goan?
– Barz a toullic, barz
an douar
Da gortoz an amzer clouar.
"– Hey, dwarf ! Ho !
"In winter where do you go?
"– In my hole underground,
"'Til the warm days come around."[120]

Heaps of dwarves

There are countless types of dwarves, and it is almost impossible to list them all. Nevertheless, we must mention the berstucs, minute dwarves of Slavic origin, who are sometimes discovered by workers, asleep under mounds of earth or hidden under blades of grass. Curètes are a type of gnome, servants of Rhea, living on the isle of Crete. They made noise with their weapons to mask the cries of the infant Zeus and prevent him from being discovered by his father Chronos. Dactyles, from the Greek word *dactylos*, "finger", are phrygian gnomes with exceptionally agile fingers, servants of Cybele, and who are credited with the invention of metalwork. The goetes are evil gnomes and witches from Bohemia; Ismaël Mérindol mentioned them living near the castle of Vyserhad ("the towering castle") on the right bank of the River Vltava in Prague, and who have the sinister speciality of forging bewitched shoes of steel. Gommes from the Vaud Alpes, related to kobolds and knockers, are the guardian dwarves of underground mines. Trows from the Shetland and Orkney Isles are blacksmiths and metallurgists. And the myrmidons, sons of Myrmex, the young maiden transformed into an ant by Athena, who consequently never grow taller than an ant themselves.

119. Walter Map, *De Nugis Curialium*, London, 1924.
120. René-François Le Men, *Traditions et superstitions de la Basse-Bretagne*, Revue celtique, 1870–1872.

Nibelung

Niflungars

The nibelung are a race of chthonian dwarves, their name meaning "sons of the mist", who are subjects of King Niebelung. They are guardians of an immense treasure seized by the hero Siegfried in the *Song of the Niebelungen*, a thirteenth-century epic based on ancient sources, which served as inspiration for Richard Wagner's famous tetralogy *Der Ring des Neibelungen* (The Ring Cycle).

According to the original legend, a dispute arose between the two sons of King Niebelung, Schilbung and Niebelung, regarding the treasure inherited from their father. The hero Siegfried helped them divide it up. To reward him, the dwarves gave him the magic sword Balmung, which had belonged to the king himself. But Siegfried seized the sword and slit the throats of the two dwarves, then reduced the seven hundred warriors of the Nibelung kingdom to slavery. He encountered hostility from Alberich, the rebel dwarf, who sought vengeance by killing the hero; but Siegfried succeeded in snatching away Alberich's veil of invisibility, and thus remained the uncontested master of the treasure. In his adaptation, Wagner drew very loosely on this original plot, and emphasised the treachery of the Nibelung, while portraying Siegfried as a pure and blameless hero.

Niflungar

Pygmies

This term was coined by the colonials, and is still commonly used to designate the Binga, Mbuti and Twa peoples of central Africa, who obviously do not refer to

themselves by this name. The word "pygmy" originated in Greek mythology. Pygmies, aboriginal tribes of small stature from Lapland, Latvia and Finland, were mentioned by Aristotle and also by Homer, who described how they attacked the sleeping Hercules after he conquered the giant Anteus. Startled, the hero reacted by rolling the pygmies in his cape. Karl Grün also refers to them: "This tiny race was attacked by troops of cranes on the seashore. So they solemnly mounted their steeds of rams and billy-goats, armed themselves with spears, and thus managed to send the

cranes scurrying. They lived in hollows in the ground, their carts were drawn by partridges, and they were so small they used hatchets to reap their wheat. Their womenfolk were old at eight, and they gave birth at the age of three to five."[121] Fearing the eastern Asae invaders, the pygmies fled into exile in western Europe and, in particular, the Celtic countries. Because of their small size, their excellent skills in metallurgy, and their knowledge of magic and potions, they came to be identified with the legendary dwarves, in the manner described by partisans of the "pygmy theory".

PYGMY THEORY

During the nineteenth century many writers defended the "pygmy theory", the staunchest of whom was Sir Walter Scott, who declared: "In fact, there seems reason to conclude that these duergar were originally nothing else than the diminutive natives of the Lappish, Lettish, and Finnish nations, who, flying before the conquering weapons of the Asae, sought the most retired regions of the north, and there endeavoured to hide themselves from their Eastern

invaders."[122] David MacRitchie[123] considered them to be a prehistoric Mongolian tribe who penetrated into Europe from the north of Scotland. Driven out by the Celtic tribes, they chose to live a troglodytic existence, thus giving rise to legends peopled by underground- and cave-dwelling

dwarves. According to Jacob Grimm, "the retreat of the dwarves in the face of advancing human civilisation gives the impression of a conquered race."[124] Another folklore scholar, Walter Johnson, considers that the legends associated with dwarves are, "to a large extent, an obvious reminder in popular memory of a little race of mysterious people, who embraced magic, and who, in the minds of the Celts, were the original inhabitants of that island."[125] The writer Arthur Machen also

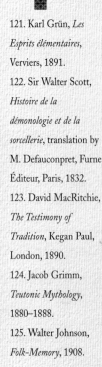

Pygmies are descendants of a prehistoric tribe of mongolian origin.

121. Karl Grün, *Les Esprits élémentaires*, Verviers, 1891.

122. Sir Walter Scott, *Histoire de la démonologie et de la sorcellerie*, translation by M. Defauconpret, Furne Éditeur, Paris, 1832.

123. David MacRitchie, *The Testimony of Tradition*, Kegan Paul, London, 1890.

124. Jacob Grimm, *Teutonic Mythology*, 1880–1888.

125. Walter Johnson, *Folk-Memory*, 1908.

People' as being the small, dark-skinned aboriginals who fled from the invading Celts around 1500 to 1000 BC."[126]

EARTH SPIRITS

A sixteenth-century book of magic likens the pygmies to gnomes living in the entrails of the earth, or else to friendly genies under the control of sorcerers: "Pygmies are earth spirits. They live underground and are subjects of their Commander-in-Chief, the great Prince Marbuel, followed by Prince Buruel and, finally, King Urinaphton. They are peace-loving souls, and far from harming mankind, they enjoy his company."[127]

gives credit to this "pygmy theory" in his fantasy novels about the Little People: "Even today, at Antrim, people can show you where these dwellings may be found, and will tell you that fairies lived there. And nine times out of ten, you can be sure they are telling the truth, as long as you accept the definition of 'fairies' or 'Little

126. Arthur Machen,
Le Petit Peuple, 1927,
translated from English
by Norbert Gaulard in
*Chroniques du Petit
Peuple*, Terre de Brume,
1998.
127. Dr Johannes Faust,
*Magia Naturalis et
Innaturalis, oder
Dreifacher Höllenzwang*,
Passau, 1505.

Orcs or Picts?

The orcs described by J.R.R. Tolkien in *The Lord of the Rings* as being elves gone astray, are most likely derived from the "pygmy theory". Their name comes from the word *Orkein*, a Norse name for the Orkney Isles, to the north of Scotland, mentioned in Scandinavian sagas. They are reminiscent of the indigenous tribes who were rather frightening, being small blue-skinned creatures covered in hair, and living underground, from whence they sprang like devils. At the time of the first Viking invasions (around 600 AD), the original inhabitants of the Orkneys, and of Scotland in general, were the Picts, as the Romans called them, because they painted their skin blue before going into battle. Or else they wore tattoos, like many Celts, and lived in *crannog*, huts half-buried by earth to resist the elements. The Picts were conquered by the scots ("pirates") who came from Ireland beginning around 500 AD, and founded the Scottish people. Possibly they were the last of this pre-Celtic pygmy tribe discussed above ✦

STONE AND RUIN DWELLERS

Red caps

Bonnets rouges, bloody bonnets

These fearsome dwarves from the Scottish Highlands resemble little old grey-haired men with plaited beards, eagle claws instead of hands, long teeth and glowing red eyes. They are found in the ruins of old castles, where their preferred lairs are on top of crumbling towers and keeps. From these heights they lie in wait for innocent hikers whom they fear may invade their domain, and they throw heavy rocks down to crush them.

Shod with steel boots, they carry a pikestaff, and dip their red caps in the fresh blood of their victims to revive the colour.[128]

To chase red caps away, all you need is to show the symbol of the cross, which they abhor; at this they flee, leaving behind one of their long fangs.

It is said that the ignoble Lord Soulis, from Hermitage castle, managed to tame a red cap, who protected him from his enemies and prevented any weapons from harming him.

Finally, to kill Soulis, his enemies had to plunge him into a cauldron of boiling oil.

Korrigans

Horned men, korrils, kourils, korred, kornikaned, cornicanets, poulpikans, poulpiquets, korandons, kornandons, kouricans, kérions, corics, courils, teuz

Korrigans are dwarves living exclusively in the Finistère and Côtes-d'Armor regions of Brittany. Their

*Illustration:
© Sandrine Gestin*

*Red
caps,
bloody
bonnets*

128. William Henderson, *Folk-Lore of the Northern Countries*, London, 1879.

Horned men,
korrils, kourils,
korred,
kornikaned,
cornicanets,
poulpikans,
poulpiquets,
korandons,
kornandons,
kouricans,
kérions, corics,
courils, teuz

129. Corentin Tranois,
Coricanets, "Revue de
Bretagne", tome IV,
Rennes, 1834.
130. Paul Sébillot,
*Croyances, mythes et
légendes des pays de
France, Le Monde
souterrain,*
(1904–1906),
Omnibus, 2002.
131. Émile Souvestre,
"Les korrils de
Plaudren", *Le Foyer
breton*, Paris, 1844.

name is derived from the Breton *korr* or *korig*, "dwarf", and is seen in certain common French family names such as Le Corre.

Swarthy-skinned and covered with a shock of frizzy hair, they have a large head from which sprout two small horns; they are clothed in green sackcloth. Their dark (sometimes red) beady little eyes glitter in their sockets. Their hands are equipped with cats' claws and their feet are covered with goathorn. Their bellowing voices resound from the depths of the earth. Male korrigans wear a large flat hat trimmed with a velvet ribbon, while the female korriganed don violet bonnets. Tucked into their belts they have a small horn which they blow into, a leather purse filled with gold, and another strange little bag. According to Corentin Tranois, Headmaster of the *lycée* at Saint-Brieuc: "As you know, the cornicanets have little canvas bags similar to a beggar's sack; in these they carry horsehair plucked from the mane and tail, and a pair of scissors. I know not what they do with these little bundles, but they never lose sight of them, except when they get up to dance."[129] In fact, this horsehair changes into rivers of stones and into priceless jewels. That is why the korrigans watch over their canvas bags very closely.

THE KORRIGAN'S HOUSE

Korrigans live amongst rocks, under menhirs or inside dolmens, known in Lower Brittany as *ty-corriked*, "dwarves' houses", or *loch-corri-ganed*, "dwarves lodges", which they carefully sweep out each day.

Paul Sébillot reports that in Lower Brittany "the *kouril* kingdom extends far underground, deeper than the seas and rivers, and the interior of the globe contains a tribe known as the cornadons."[130] Despite their tiny size, korrigans are endowed with herculean strength and magical powers, which enabled them to introduce dolmens into Brittany by transporting them on their backs. Magicians and clairvoyants, they are able to find buried treasure. In spite of their surly looks and irritable nature, they are able to carry out household tasks, as long as one is careful to leave small offerings about the house for them, or have a flat stone near the hearth for them to sit and warm themselves. Otherwise, they will play a thousand abominable tricks such as untying the cattle at night, sewing sleepers into their sheets, or stealing babes from their cribs and leaving their own ugly progeniture in their place, like changelings.

KORRIGAN CLANS

Émile Souvestre distinguishes different clans of korrigans: "Those who live in the woods were called *kornikaneds*, because they sang into little horns which they hung from their belts; those who live on the moors were called *korrils*, because they spent each night dancing around in the moonlight; and those who lived in the valleys were *poulpikans*, 'with burrows in the low country'." [131]

INCORRIGIBLE KORRILS

The korrils haunting the low-lying Landes spend entire nights dancing around menhirs and other standing stones. Any unfortunate victim who gets caught up in their round must dance until he drops, sometimes to the death. Unless perchance, as in the tale of *The Two Hunchbacks*, he is able to recite the end of the rhyme about the days of the week, for they only know the beginning, (Monday, Tuesday, Wednesday, etc.) But should the victim succeed, they will reward him by offering him the choice between beauty or riches.
René-François Le Men relates

Illustration:
© Sandrine Gestin

the perils of this nocturnal dance: "One of the dwarves' favourite pastimes is dancing in the moonlight around a huge bonfire. In the desolate Landes region they can be seen dancing frenziedly, and singing the first words of a little verse they are prohibited from finishing themselves. What is more, it seems that there is more rhyme than reason to this chorus, which consists simply of chanting the first few days of the week. This is how they sing it:

"Dissul,
"Dilun,
"Dimeurs ha dimerc'her,
"Diriaou ha dirguener.

"Sunday,
"Monday,
"Tuesday and Wednesday,
"Thursday and Friday.

"Should a passer-by have the misfortune to come across them during their dancing and revelry on the moors, they call him by name, and if he replies, he is caught up in their frenzied whirling, and continues until he drops dead on the ground."[132]
At the close of the eighteenth century, Jacques Cambry, Public Prosecutor of Lorient and President of the Celtic Academy, published this account of the

132. René-François Le Men, *Traditions et superstitions de la Basse-Bretagne*, Revue celtique, 1870–1872.
133. Jacques Cambry, *Voyage dans le Finistère*, 1799, reprint, Brest, 1836.
134. Paul Sébillot, *Croyances, mythes et légendes des pays de France, La Mer*, (1904–1906), Omnibus, 2002.

sinister korrils: "During my investigation at Tresmalaouen, while I was studying these curious ruins, I saw a shepherd sitting nearby; I asked him what the locals thought of this ancient monu-ment, and he repeated what I had already been told. That it was the

palace of the Courils or little men, a nasty type of corrupt, dancing sorcerer. They can be seen in the moonlight, bounding around sacred stones or druidic monuments. Should they grab you by the hand, you must follow their movements; then they go, leaving you lying exhausted on the ground."[133] Korandons dance near the cave that bears their name, in Portsmoguer cove, in Lower Brittany. Instead of legs they have steel-shod goat's feet. "At night they dance noisily, and the sound of the pebbles shifting as the waves break on the shore has been at-tributed to the clatter of their

steel shoes."[134] Ismaël Mérindol reported similar tales in the sixteenth century. They are not korrils, which are only found in Brittany, but feline sorcerers. As we know, the korrigans have cats' claws on their hands, which seems to corroborate a relationship between the korrigans and the catlike people. The author of *Traité de Faërie* described the rounds of these cat sorcerers, as he witnessed them with his own eyes in his youth: "Cats danced around in circles in the moonlight, on their hind legs and with their forepaws joined, caterwauling like things pos-sessed. Their eyes glowed red, proof – if any were needed– that the demon himself was leading the dance. I crouched down, my nose in the laven-der, and watched this catty choregraphy. But I took care not to draw any closer, for the cats would never have let me go alive. I was only eight years old, but already I knew the limits of Fairylore beyond which I must not venture."[135]

plough-cleaning fork (*see illustration*). For someone forced to dance against his will, René-François Le Men also suggests the method consisting of "placing his clogs in the ring in such a way that after the first round of dancing he can put both feet into them at once."[136] He may also "plant a stick in the ground at the spot where he began dancing, and seize hold of it as he finishes the first round."[137]

goatherds searching for their lost animals. The *teuz ar pouliet*, or "pond prankster", is a little dwarf dressed in green with fine gaiters, who can become invisible at will or adopt any shape at all.[138]

HOW TO BE RID OF THEM

To avoid the traps which these terrible korrils set, it is advisable to always carry some religious object, such as a cross, crucifix, missal, rosary beads, saint's medallion or vial of holy water, or else a few leaves of verbena. Émile Souvestre recommends a small

DISGUSTING POULPIKANS

Poulpikans, or poulpiquets, like the teuz, are a type of korrigan who rummage around in foul places – "*fouillent*" (pikan) in "*lieux bas*" (poul). They are found in ponds, bog holes, swamps and even in latrines. They play dirty tricks on humans; for example, they ring imaginary bells to deceive

135. Ismaël Mérindol, *Traité de Faërie*, 1466.
136 and 137. René-François Le Men, *Traditions et superstitions de la Basse-Bretagne*, Revue celtique, 1870–1872.
138. Émile Souvestre, "Les korrils de Plaudren", *Le Foyer breton*, Paris, 1844.

The korrils of Plaudren

"In Plaudren, near the hamlet of Loqueltas, there was a moor called *Motten-Dervenn* (or as the Galots say, "the land of the oaks"), where there was a large village of korrils which is still there today. These nasty dwarves went there to dance every night, and whoever ventured on the moors was sure to be drawn into their circle and forced to twirl around with them until the first cock's crow; so none dared go there.

"But one evening Bénéad Guilcher was returning with his wife from a field where he had been ploughing all day for a farmer from Cadoudal, and they took a shortcut across the haunted moor. It was still early, and they hoped that the korrigans would not yet have begun their dancing; but as they reached the centre of the Motten-Dervenn, they saw them scattered around the large stones, like birds in a field of wheat. They were about to turn back when the horns of the forest dwarves and the calls of the valley dwarves rang out behind them. Bénéad felt his legs tremble beneath him, and said to his wife:

"'Saint Anne! All is lost, for here are the kornikaneds and the poulpikans who have come to join the korrils, and carouse all night long. They will force us to dance until dawn, and my poor old heart will not withstand it.'

"In fact, hordes of korrigans arrived from all sides, surrounding Guilcher and his wife like wasps around a honey pot; but they backed away when they spied the small plough cleaning implement that Bénéad was holding, and they all began to sing in unison:

"*Lez-hi, lez-hon,*
"*Bac'h an arèr zo gant hon;*
"*Lez-on, lez-hi,*
"*Bac'h an arèr zo gant hi.*

"Let them walk free,
"A plough fork has he!
"Let her be, let him bide,
"The fork's on their side.

"Straight away Guilcher understood that the stick he was carrying was a magic weapon against the korrigans, and he passed between them with his other half and suffered no ill.

"This served as a warning to the villagers. From that day on, everyone went abroad at night with a little fork, and was able to cross the heath without fear." [139]

139. Émile Souvestre, "Les korrils de Plaudren", *Le Foyer breton*, Paris, 1844.

The hill people

-5-

The hill people are the most troublesome of all in Fairyland.

They include the large tribe of imps, consisting of numerous families spread throughout Europe, all of whom are more or less related. From the jovial Irish cluricaunes and leprechauns to the mysterious Breton bugel-noz; from the helpful nutons of Wallony to the mocking pucks of the English forests, they are to be found in all climes. With time, many of them have settled into family homes, where they carry out various domestic tasks. But whether they be Anglo-Saxon brownies, Breton imps, Swiss servants or nisses and tomtes from the Far North, they are all capable of playing nasty tricks if you ignore them.

FROM THE HILLS

Boggarts

*Bogies, bogles, bugs (England),
bwca (Wales)*

Boggarts are hideous, hairy dwarfish creatures who are perfectly evil in their dealings with humans. They haunt the English moors, and are often responsible for destroying thatched-roof cottages. They are the degenerate cousins of the gentle brownies. While the latter have been domesticated for a long time, and have become the amiable servants of the household, dwarves have never evolved beyond their original wild state. They are closely related to the German poltergeist.

King James I of England, author of a famous work on demonology, printed in London in 1597, speaks of "a hairy fellow who haunts various homes without doing any ill, but sometimes behaves as if it were necessary to turn the whole house upside down." He kicks madly at the walls, throws crockery around, or tortures the sleepers by pinching them.

The only way to get rid of them is through exorcism.

Untamed bwcas are in the habit of walking for hours on end in streams, or traipsing through mudpuddles, hence their name "puddlefoot". Once they get into family homes, they leave behind them muddy, wet trails which irritate the housekeepers.

HOW TO GET RID OF THEM

These hot-tempered little creatures will flee if someone guesses their name, which they like to keep secret. Once, a farm maid kept a bwca who spun wool for her during the night. Several times she asked him his name, but he never replied. One night she spied on him while he was working, and she heard him singing softly:

*Ah! that scullery maid,
would she
[mock me not,
If she knew that my name
[is Gwarwyn-a-throt!*

The girl laughed out loud, and emerging from the shadows, began to repeat over and over the name she had just heard. Mad with rage, the bwca ran off into the night, never to return.

Bugel-noz

This "night-time shepherd" is a Breton imp and prankster who gets up to a thousand and one tricks during *fest-noz*, or evening festivities. He also appears at crossroads, where he changes shape and size enormously: "His gigantic size increases the closer one gets to his shadow. The bugel-noz covers himself with a white cloak which trails on the ground behind him. They say that he only shows himself to travellers who delay into the night, and who thus need protection

*Illustration:
© Sandrine Gestin*

Cluricaunes

MONEY COUNTERFEITERS

from the works of the devil. He approaches the vulnerable traveller and enfolds him in the cloak, which protects him from all danger. The devil loses all his power at the sight of the bugel-noz, and runs off uttering blood-curdling screams: his raging fury echoes in the distance, amidst the terrible clatter of his cart, flying through space like an arrow, and leaving behind a trail of blinding light and foul-smelling fumes."[140]

Cluricaunes are Irish spirits in the form of little old men fifteen centimetres tall. They wear a long red cloak secured with a large silver clasp, blue stockings, high-heeled, buckled shoes, and a red nightcap. They are cousins of the leprechauns, but while the latter are cantankerous and hard working, the cluricaunes are happy-go-lucky.

Unlike the wealthy leprechauns, cluricaunes are destitute. But they make up for this by manufacturing their own currency, which has no value in the human context, and is disdainfully rejected as counterfeit money. Sometimes the hills ring with the sound of their hammers striking their false coins. Reverend Kirk confirms this: "Even English writers relate of Barry Island in Glamorganshyre that laying your ear unto a cleft of the Rock; blowing of Bellows,

Painting: The party, *early 20th century, private collection, © Giraudon/ Bridgeman Art Library*

140. Vérusmor, *Voyage en Basse-Bretagne,* Jollivet, Guingamp, 1855.

striking of hammers, clashing of armour, filing of irons will be heard distinctly, ever since Merlin enchanted those subterranean Wights, forcing them to forge with their own hands the arms for Aurelius Ambrosius and his Brittains, till he returned; which Merlin being killed in batell, and not coming to undo this spell, these active Vulcans are there condemned to a perpetuall labour."[141]

SECRETS OF WHISKEY

Having a liking for the bottle, the cluricaunes have gradually left their hills and taken up residence in human wine-cellars, where they tipple from the bottles; naturally, they seek out serious drinkers who have well-stocked cellars. They are particularly troublesome in pubs, where they drain kegs of Guiness or Kilkenny in next to no time – particularly on Saint-Patrick's Day!
It is also said that we owe the original recipe for authentic Irish whiskey to these dwarves, who distilled it three times instead of twice as for Scotch whisky. Long ago, being tired of haunting the damp moors of Ireland, and racked with rheumatism, they asked the Irish for permission to reside part time in their cellars, in exchange for which they would offer them treasure. The residents of the Emerald Isle readily accepted, for they thought the cluricaunes very wealthy – little did they realize that their wealth was nothing more than gimcrack. The treasure in question glowed like gold, but tasted quite different: it was whiskey! But the Irish did not lose on their deal, and even today, they leave offerings to their good friends the cluricaunes by spilling a few drops of whiskey from their glasses on the pub counter!

Fir darrig

Far darrig, fir dhearga

The fir darrig of Ireland are nicknamed the "red men" after the colour of their vests and caps. They are cousins of the leprechauns and cluricaunes.
The fir darrig from Donegal is a gigantic imp. On the other hand, the fir darrig of Munster is a little wizened man standing

seventy-five centimetres tall, with long grey hair and dressed entirely in red. Should he come knocking at the door, asking to be allowed to sit by the fireside, it is best to let him in, for the fir darrig are very quick to harass humans and play outrageous tricks on them.
Thomas Keightley relates a nineteenth-century account of how a fir darrig came to seek shelter in a cabin where there lived a man and his daughter. The stranger was a little old

Far darrig, fir dhearga

141. Robert Kirk, *Secret Commonwealth*, 1691, edited by S. Sanderson, D.S. Brewer, 1976.

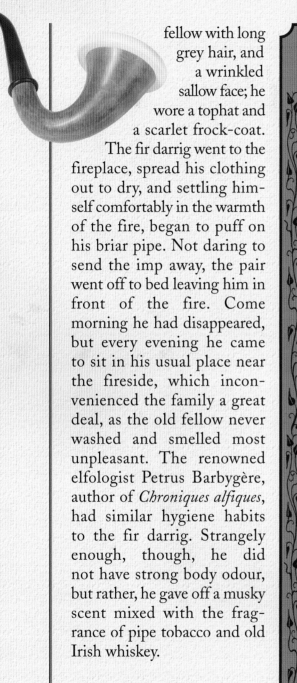

fellow with long grey hair, and a wrinkled sallow face; he wore a tophat and a scarlet frock-coat.

The fir darrig went to the fireplace, spread his clothing out to dry, and settling himself comfortably in the warmth of the fire, began to puff on his briar pipe. Not daring to send the imp away, the pair went off to bed leaving him in front of the fire. Come morning he had disappeared, but every evening he came to sit in his usual place near the fireside, which inconvenienced the family a great deal, as the old fellow never washed and smelled most unpleasant. The renowned elfologist Petrus Barbygère, author of *Chroniques alfiques*, had similar hygiene habits to the fir darrig. Strangely enough, though, he did not have strong body odour, but rather, he gave off a musky scent mixed with the fragrance of pipe tobacco and old Irish whiskey.

Hobbits, Smurfs and other Lilliputians

Among the many families comprising the Little People of the hills, there are several other groups, born from the imagination of writers and comic-strip creators.

Thus, the hobbits only exist in the works of J.R.R. Tolkien: *Bilbo the Hobbit* and *The Lord of the Rings*. Smaller than dwarves, they are about ninety centimetres tall on average. Their most outstanding physical characteristic is their feet, with soles like leather and covered with a thick layer of brown fur, which is why they never wear shoes. Happy-go-lucky, peace-loving creatures who live from day to day, they have a wide face with rosy round cheeks and their eyes are usually blue. They tend to be rather chubby (as they eat up to six meals a day) and live up to a hundred years. They are naturally sedentary creatures, and like nothing more than to stay in their underground warrens, which they arrange as cosy "home sweet homes". They pass hours on end just smoking their pipes, filled with a secret substance known only to them.

The Smurfs are minute dwarves from the Middle Ages, created by the comic strip artist Peyo in 1958 in his work *The Smurfs and the Magic Flute*, an album relating the adventures of Johan and Pirlouit (Peewit). Their skin is blue, they are no bigger than an apple, with a short tail, and wear short trousers and a white cap. Their chief, Papa Smurf, sports a white beard, and red trousers and cap. The Smurfs live in a mushroom village in a cursed country where the inhabitants speak the Smurf language: "A Smurf who speaks Smurf without his Smurf is a good Smurf."

Lilliputians were a race of tiny dwarves from the kingdom of Lilliput, popularised by Jonathan Swift in *Gulliver's Travels* (1726). They measured less than fifteen centimetres high. They were divided into two tribes: those with high heels and others with flat-heeled shoes. The Lilliputians were involved in all manner of intrigues, and formed a faction known as Little-endians, who spent their time warring with the Big-endians, from the neighbouring island of Blefescu. The Lilliputians succeeded in tying Gulliver down to the ground using thin cords, but in the end they expelled him from Lilliput after he urinated on the royal palace to extinguish a fire. 🝔

Leprechauns

Leprechauns are cobbler imps about ninety centimetres high, who live in the Irish coppices, especially under medlar trees. They hail from the northern part of Leinster, and are related to the cluricaunes of Cork, the luricaunes of Kerry, the lurigadaunes of Tipperary, the lurachmains or loghery men of Ulster, the luricans of Connaught and the lurgadhans of Munster. But the leprechauns are so popular that their name is known throughout Ireland.[142] They are also cousins of the fir darrig.

Cobbler imps

Generally rather surly and bad-tempered, leprechauns avoid contact with humans. This is rather easy for them, given their fleetness of foot: they move so quicky that their image does not even have time to register on the retina of the human eye. In winter they hibernate, and do not reappear until the warmer weather returns.

These solitary little old fellows dress in green jackets, red buckled shoes and woollen stockings, and a small leather apron. They top all this off with a tricorn hat, the brim turned up on one side. They smoke a pipe called a "dudeen", and are rather partial to their own home-distilled whiskey, or "poteen". Female leprechauns do not exist, and nothing is known of their reproduction methods.

Their name is derived from the Gaelic *leith*, "half", and *bhrogan*, "shapeless old clod-hoppers". In fact, they are called "one-shoed cobblers" because, for some reason, leprechauns only resole one shoe, and never the pair. On summer evenings in the Irish countryside the joyful sounds of their little hammers can be clearly heard. Their name may also come from the Irish *luarcharma'n*, meaning "pygmy".

THE LITTLE PEOPLE'S BANKERS

Traditionally, leprechauns are the guardians of valuable treasures, which they stash away in their imp kingdom under enchanted hillocks. They are considered to be the bankers of the Little People of Ireland.

If you are lucky enough to catch a leprechaun, you can release him in exchange for his fortune. But beware: leprec-

hauns are crafty; they will tell a thousand lies and invent a thousand tricks to avoid giving anything in exchange.

Once a farmer from Kerry discovered a leprechaun dozing in his field; he grabbed him by the goatee and demanded that he hand over his treasure. The dwarf

Leprechauns only ever replace the sole on one shoe, never the pair.

142. Bob Curran, *Guide pratique des esprits irlandais*, Appletree Press, 1997 and Katharine Briggs, *A Dictionary of Fairies*, Penguin Books, London, 1976.

the lucky recipient can never use it, for the coin very soon changes into leaves or ashes.

sobbed, threatened, promised, lied and finally revealed the hiding place: the treasure was at the foot of a ragwort, in the middle of a field covered with many of these plants. The farmer released the dwarf, knotted a red belt around the plant and went home to get a spade. On his return, imagine his surprise to discover that every ragwort in the field had a red belt attached to it, identical to his own!

Nuitons, sotês

THE LUCKY SHILLING

Leprechauns also wear at their waist two small leather pouches. In the first is a "lucky shilling", a magic coin which is replaced as soon as it is spent. In this way, the leprechaun can buy anything his heart desires, by paying with shillings. In the second purse he carefully keeps a gold coin which he gives away in emergencies. But

143. Albert Doppagne, *Esprits et génies du terroir*, Duculot, 1977.

Nutons

Nuitons, sotês

Nutons are artisan imps living in Wallony, in Southern Belgium, where they are very well liked. With their white beards, pointed caps and green suits, they are the stars of the carnival of Malmedy, where nuton masks are worn. They live in caves called "nuton caves" or "sote holes", and at nightfall, peasants leave outside broken dishes, dented saucepans, shoes for resoling, socks to be darned or dirty laundry, along with morsels of food such as a cup of milk or a

chunk of bread. In turn, the nuton launderers, weavers, cobblers, blacksmiths or tinkers work throughout the night, repairing, polishing, darning, laundering, and scrubbing. By morning, when the peasants rise, the articles left out the night before are there, shining like new, and the food has disappeared. "A blacksmith had not had time to finish a wheel which he had to deliver the next day. Not knowing how to overcome this problem, he thought of leaving the unfinished wheel near the entrance to the nutons' cave, along with some tasty titbits. Next morning, the wheel was finished, and ready to be delivered."[143]

THE VENGEANCE OF THE NUTONS

Though most obliging, nutons are nevertheless very sensitive, and seek cruel revenge on humans who scorn their services. A farmer, fearing the approach of a storm, was hurrying to get his wheat into the barn. A well-meaning nuton offered to help, but brought the wheat in ear by ear. The farmer, irritated by this, told the nuton to clear off. Hurt by this, he retorted:

Ear by ear, I made you rich,
Sheaf by sheaf, I'll ruin you!

Instantaneously, the farmer's crop was ruined, then his stables and house were dam-aged by the storm and then by fire.[144]

Illustration: © Sandrine Gestin

Pixies

Piskies, pisgy, pixy, pix, pics, picts

Pixies are untamed imps living in the south-west of England, especially in the forests of Devon, Somerset, Dartmoor, Exmoor and East Hampshire. They are said to be descended from the Red Heads, the first inhabitants of Cornwall, but their name is also related to the Picts, people living in Scotland before the Scot invasion around 500 AD (see "pygmy-theory", p. 98).

Pixies look like red-headed boys, with cute but insolent, freckled little faces, snub noses and squinty eyes; when they aren't naked they are dressed in green, and are well known for their mischievous nature. But their physical characteristics vary from region to region. The folklore specialist Katharine Briggs writes: "The Cornish piskie is older, more wizened and thinner than the sturdy down-to-earth Somerset pixy, and the slender, fine, white-complexioned pixies from Devon."[145] Their close ties with the Red Heads also mean they are related to the meryons or red-coloured "ant-fairies", which are sacred creatures in the forests where pixies dwell. It is also said that they are the wandering souls of infants who have died unbaptised. They are hostile to the fairies, with whom they are perpetually at war.

Pixies are given to teasing and tormenting humans. They upset horses all night long, curdle milk and cause cows to die, steal eggs from the hen house, take the best wines from the cellar, kiss girls on the neck and, as do the fairies with their change-lings, leave their horrible offspring, the killcrops, in place of human infants. At night they dance around in magic circles known as galli-traps, or "heel traps", for whoever ventures into one by mistake finds himself instantly transfixed by the pixies. At each one of these pranks, they burst into gales of proverbial laughter: in the south of England, "to laugh like a pixie" means to laugh excessively.

144. Albert Doppagne, *Esprits et génies du terroir*, Duculot, 1977.
145. Katharine Briggs, *A Dictionary of Fairies*, Penguin Books, London, 1976.

Piskies, pisgy, pixy, pix, pics, picts

LED ASTRAY BY THE PIXIES

It is also said that the pixies lead travellers astray in the forest, and cause them to go in circles; in such cases their victims have been "pixie-led". To avoid this kind of spell, it is important to carry one of these items, which are the only things capable of keeping the pixies at bay: a cross made of sorb wood, a horse shoe, a chunk of bread or a sack of salt. The spirits of Fairyland fear these things more than any other and, in particular, symbols of Christianity such as the crucifix, baptismal salt, and the communion host. Otherwise, another way is to turn your coat, or the lining of your pockets inside out, for – like all creatures in Fairyland – pixies have no understanding of the wrong side of things.

Once, while travelling through the English forests on foot, Ismaël Mérindol found himself pixie-led. He had been to visit the monks in the monastery of Glastonbury, which was at that time under a Celtic orthodox bishop, and which had been responsible since the fifteenth century for guarding the relics of Arthur, king of the Bretons. Despite his extensive knowledge of Fairyland, Mérindol finally had to concede that he

To escape from the pixies, you must turn your jacket, or the pockets, inside out

had been walking in circles for hours and was at risk of remaining a prisoner for ever in this enchanted forest. Then he spied the faces of some snivelling, squinting brats with buck teeth and pointed ears, peering at him through the thicket. Then he heard their laughter, like horses whinnying. So he stripped himself bare,

and then dressed again, putting his clothes on inside out. Immediately the pixies ceased their laughter and looked quite disconcerted. For by turning his vest and trousers inside out in this way, Master Mérindol had quite simply become invisible to them. No longer threatened by their intrigues, he quickly found his path and was able to get out of the bewitched forest. Nor did he adjust his clothing until that evening, once safely in the room where he was to spend the night. Needless to say, the hotel keeper was most surprised to see this important personage dressed in such a strange get-up!

Pucks

Robin-good-fellow, pooka, pwca (Wales), puckle, phuka

Pucks are evil imps found in the forests of England. They are so widespread and common that they have given their name to Puck, the main character in William Shakespeare's play *A Midsummer Night's Dream* (1595) and to Rudyard Kipling's *Puck of Pook's Hill* (1906). In fact, the name Puck comes from pwca or pooka, Welsh imps related to will-o'-the-wisps. They guard flocks in exchange for a bowl of milk or a crust of bread, but they are capable of playing all kinds of unpleasant tricks if they are not treated with respect. Richard Price of Brecon, a friend of Shakespeare, actually lived near Cwm Pwca, favourite village of the pwca. It is thought that the stories he told to the English playwright contributed to Shakespeare's development of the character Puck.

THE BUFFOON AT THE FAIRIES' COURT

Sir Walter Scott describes Puck, the court jester at the court of the fairy king: "The constant attendant upon the English Fairy court was the celebrated Puck, or Robin Goodfellow, who to the elves acted in some measure as the jester or clown of the company (a character then to be found in the establishment of every person of quality) or to use a more modern comparison, resembled the Pierrot of the pantomime ... to mislead a peasant on his path homeward, to disguise himself like a stool, in order to induce an old gossip to sit down on the floor when she expected to repose on a chair, were his special enjoyments. If he condescended to do some work for the sleeping family, in which he had some resemblance to the Scottish household spirit called a brownie, the selfish Puck was far from practising this labour on the disinterested principle of the northern goblin, who, if raiment or food was left in his way and for his use, departed from the family in displeasure. Robin Goodfellow, on the contrary, must have both his food and his rest."[146]
Reginald Scot, on the other hand, likens Puck to the hobgoblins, or English household imps, and represents them as demons feared by the people: "Know ye this, by the way, that heretofore, Robin Goodfellow and Hobgoblin were as terrible, and also as credible, to the people as hags and witches be now; and in time to come a witch will be as much derided and condemned, and as clearly perceived, as the illusion and knavery of Robin Goodfellow, upon whom there have gone as many and as credible tales as witchcraft, saving that it hath not pleased the translators of the Bible to call spirits by the name of Robin Goodfellow, as they have diviners, soothsayers, poisoners, and cozeners by the name of witches."[147]

Robin-good-fellow, pooka, pwca, puckle, phuka

146. Sir Walter Scott, *Histoire de la démonologie et de la sorcellerie*, translation by M. Defauconpret, Furne Éditeur, Paris, 1832.
147. Reginald Scot, *The Discovery of Witchcraft*, cited by Sir Walter Scott, *Histoire de la démonologie et de la sorcellerie*, translation by M. Defauconpret, Furne Éditeur, Paris, 1832.

Painting:
Puck, *1789, Sir Joshua
Reynolds (1723–1792),
oil on canvas, private
collection,
© Giraudon/Bridgeman
Art Library*

Puck was
the Jester
at the fairy
court

Thousands of imps

There are so many types and families of imps that it is difficult to try to cite them all, especially because new ones appear from time to time. But we cannot overlook the *danser-noz*, "dancers of the night", who spend all night dancing in the forest; the *fouleurs*, or "grape treaders", untamed imps who trample nightmarishly on the stomach of sleepers; the *hurleurs*, *crieurs*, *appeleurs* and *braillards*, nasty imps who cry out for help on the seashore, then drown anyone who goes to their assistance; the *jetins*, from the verb "jeter" to throw, tiny but powerful imps from the banks of the Rance River, who amuse themselves by throwing enormous stones in the fields, or playing quoits with rocks; the ugly and misshapen *sautés*, imps from the Vosges with cloven hooves, dressed in large black greatcoats, who live on farms where they clean out the stables in exchange for a bowl of milk; the *cadets* from Lyon, who yell mockingly from cellars, lofts or stables; the *feriers* of Suffolk, on the east coast of England, with their sandy-coloured skin; and lastly, the *monaciello*, or "little monk", a friendly imp from around Naples, dressed in rough homespun garb and a wide-brimmed hat. ❧

IN HOMES

Brownies

Bodagh (Scottish Highlands), bwca (Wales), fenodoree (Isle of Man)

Brownies are friendly household genies who are mainly found in Scotland, in England, in Wales and on the Isle of Man.
Physically they resemble monkeys, standing about ninety centimetres tall, without a nose, but with big blue eyes and a body completely covered with thick fur. They are always dressed in brown.

Home-loving by nature, brownies generally become attached to a family and their home, and act as their protectors. They take care of the daily household tasks, fetch the midwife when the lady of the house is about to give birth, rock in-fants in their cradle to send them off to sleep, find lost keys, advise the man of the house which cards to play at whist or which pawns to play at chess. In exchange, all they ask is for a warm spot near the fireside, and to be able to swing on a horseshoe hanging upside-down over the hearth, and which is known as a "brownies' swing".

Bodagh, Bwca, fenodoree

BROWNIES' FEASTS

For meals, all brownies need is a small glass of milk, a ladleful of cream or some bannock or cake to be left out. But beware: they can't stand bread or cake cut with a knife; it needs to be broken, otherwise they get upset. On the subject of brownie meals, one observer wrote: "They gave them little treats, their favourties being knuckled cakes made with

milled flour, toasted in the embers and drizzled with honey. The mistress of the house prepared them and carefully left them in a corner where they would find them by chance."[148] This is the origin of the cakes we nowadays call "brownies".

THE BROWNIE SERVANT

Faithful, well meaning, kindly, placid and gentle with children, brownies are nevertheless very easily hurt: the simple fact of watching while they work, or offering them new clothes is enough to upset them to the point where they will immediately leave the house never to return.

This was confirmed by Sir Walter Scott: "This spirit was easily banished, or, as it was known, hired away, by the offer of clothes or food; but many of the simple inhabitants could little see the prudence of parting with such a useful domestic drudge, who served faithfully, without fee and reward, food or raiment."[149]

Although in most cases brownies are males, there are also female brownies. One of the most famous was Meg Moulach, "Maggie the Hairy One", who was in the service of the Tullochgorum family of Strathspey in Scotland. She would bring food to the table, but all the while remaining invisible: the dishes moved through the air and landed gently on the table. She would also ensure her master won at chess. Alas, her husband, Brownie-Clod, was rather simple minded, and spent his days throwing dirt at passers-by.

Many aristocratic Scottish families, including the Mac-Douglases of Ardincaple, the MacDonalds of Largie, the MacKays of Kintyre, the Mac-Leods of Berneray and the Harrises and MacLachlans of Loch Fyne, had one or more brownies in their employ. The Doune residence at Rothiemurchus also had an excellent brownie, but he made such a noise whilst scrubbing the saucepans that the head of the house sent him packing.[150]

The brownie attached to the family of Laird Dalswinton took such good care of his daughter that not only did he facilitate her love affair with a young prince, but he also helped her undress on her wedding night, and helped her give birth after going to fetch the midwife.

Illustration:
© Sandrine Gestin

148. William Henderson, *Folk-Lore of the Northern Counties*, Folk-Lore Society, London, 1879.
149. Sir Walter Scott, *Histoire de la démonologie et de la sorcellerie*, translation by M. Defauconpret, Furne Éditeur, Paris, 1832.
150. *Minstrelsy of the Scottish Border*.

THE BREWER BROWNIES

Brownies also play an important role in the brewing of beer. In olden times it was customary to make them an offering of beer in a hollow stone called a "brownie stone", so that the household spirit could impart his perfume and his bitterness to the amber brew. But the increased spread of Christianity, which was hostile to the concept of "demons", finally caused the brownies to flee, as illustrated by this anecdote, related by Sir

Walter Scott: "Thus we are informed by Brand that a young man in the Orkneys 'used to brew, and sometimes read upon his Bible; an old woman in the house told him that Brownie was displeased with that book he read upon, and that if he continued to do so, they would get no more service out of Brownie; but the young man, being better instructed from that book, which was Brownie's eyesore and the object of his wrath, when he brewed, would not give in to Brownie's demands; whereupon the first and second brewings were spoilt, and of no use; for though the fermentation began well enough, yet in a little time it left off working, and grew cold; but from the third broust, or brewing, he had very good ale, even though he had not given in to Brownie, with whom afterwards they were no more troubled."

Another story of the same kind is told of a lady in Uist, who refused, on religious grounds, the usual sacrifice to this domestic spirit. The first and second brewings failed, but the third succeeded; and thus, when Brownie lost the perquisite to which he had been so long accustomed, he abandoned the inhospitable house, where his services had so long been faithfully rendered. The last place in the south of Scotland supposed to have been honoured, or benefited, by the residence of a Brownie, was Bodsbeck in Moffatdale.[151]

Gremlins

Gremlins are imps who are well versed in the latest mechanics and technology. Their name was first used by British aviators posted on the northwest border of India during the Second World War. They took the brandname for Fremlin's beer, and replaced the F with a G for the Grimm brothers, authors of the famous fairy tales.

Originally, gremlins were spirits who lived in aeroplane engines. Like all imps, they were real troublemakers, and took great delight in causing the engines to cut out in full flight, emptying the fuel tanks, or causing a thousand and one little things to go wrong. But they always made sure the planes got home safely, without loss of life or limb. When the

Gremlins delight in making aeroplane engines cut out in mid-flight

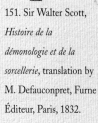

151. Sir Walter Scott, *Histoire de la démonologie et de la sorcellerie*, translation by M. Defauconpret, Furne Éditeur, Paris, 1832.

mechanics inspected the engines, the problem had always mysteriously disappeared. Since that time, the gremlins have graduated to other types of machinery, including motor vehicles, household appliances, audiovisual equipment and especially computers, whose viruses and worms are the work of gremlins in most cases. That is why it is important to get into the good books of these spirits, by leaving some tasty morsel near the computer for them: a rosebud in a glass of water, a small glass of milk or some cake crumbs is sufficient. If cajoled in this way, gremlins will stop teasing the hard disk, and for users of the Internet, they have proven to be the most effective of firewalls.

Imps

Lubins, lupins, ludions, luitons, luprons, letiens, folletti (Italy), sprites, hobgoblins (Britain), kwelgeert, plageert (Flanders)

The word "imp" refers to any small-sized creature – infinitely smaller than dwarves –

with a gleeful but mischievous nature. The term "imp" was first used in 1564, and is derived from the twelfth-century Old French *luitun*, which in turn came from the Latin *neptunus*, used in a list of demons dating from the seventh century.

Strictly speaking, imps are of French descent, and more specifically of Breton origin. But the name has now become a generic term, similar to "fairy", "dwarf" or "giant", to designate various clans and families, which are described and named differently according to the regions. For example, the fions of Brittany live on the Isle of Batz, in caves along the coast. They are related to the *tréo-fall* from the Isle of Ouessant, and the *fras* from the Isle of Yeu. In the Alps, the Jura, and the canton

of Vaud in Switzerland, *fantines, fouletots* and *niounelous* are troglodytic imps who live in holes in the rocks. They are especially skilled with cattle in the alpine pastures, and are of great assistance to the peasants. But if they are not shown due respect, they will dry up the cows' milk, set the cattle wandering, or cause travellers to lose their way. Elsewhere in Europe, the imps have other names: *folletti* in Italy, *kwelgeert* and *plageert* in Flanders. In England they are known as sprites: in the north, near the villages of Bowdin and Gateside, the cowlug sprites are endowed with huge ears like cows.

TROOPING AND SOLITARY IMPS

In the same way, imps vary, and may be untamed, living in the wild, or domesticated, such as those living in homes in England, where they are called "hobgoblins". Among the wild imps, we must draw a distinction between the trooping fairies, who live together in large numbers in underground mazes, their walls rendered with a mixture of clay, moss and sweet-smelling grasses, and always dressed in green, and their counterparts, the solitary fairies, who are easily recognisable by their red costumes.

DOMESTICATED IMPS

The majority of wild imps have gradually become sedentary, living as household imps in private homes, especially in Brittany and in England, their mother-countries.

These domesticated imps love nothing more than to bask in the warmth in front of a huge fire. In Great Britain they are called "hobgoblins" due to their liking for sitting on the hob beside the fire.

Jean de la Fontaine refers to these hobgoblins, which he calls *follets* or lively spirits, who live in "Mogol":

Within the great Mogul's domains there are Familiar sprites of much domestic use:

They sweep the house, and take a tidy care Of equipage, nor garden work refuse; But if you meddle with their toil, The whole, at once, you're sure to spoil. [152]

BRETON IMPS

In Brittany the imps feel at home, and there are numerous reports of their good and loyal service. G. le Calvez, a teacher at Caulnes, explains: "The imp is a genie in the house, or on the farm, and he may be good or bad, depending on the way he is treated.

"He is everywhere, by the hearth, in the barn, in the cellar, near the oven, by the mill, inside the *ty-koz*, or large bins where the grain is stored, on top of old cupboards, or amongst the shiny old copper pots and pans." [153]

Imps are given to taking long naps during the day; for this they sneak off to an attic or to the hayloft in the stables. But once night falls, and the household is asleep, they come out of their hiding places, scamper towards the fireplace to get warm and to eat up all the meal scraps that are left out for them, such as potato peelings, carrot tops, jugs of milk, buckwheat pancakes, and sometimes bits of bacon. Then they begin work, putting away and tidying, washing dishes, sweeping in corners, scouring pots, filling pitchers with fresh water, in short, carefully doing all the essential house-hold chores. They prevent bacon from turning rancid and milk from curdling, they bolt the flour, and glean the grain left behind in the fields by the reapers. Imps also like to imitate human activities, even though their

Mischievous imps are useful household genies

152. La Fontaine, *Fables*, "The Wishes", book VII.

153. G. Le Calvez, *Les Lutins dans le pays de Tréguer*, "Revue des traditions populaires", 1886.

Painting:
The Presentation,
Eleanor Fortescue-
Brickdale, (1871–1945),
private collection,
© *Giraudon/Bridgeman*
Art Library

efforts produce no results. Marie Cocagn, an old woman from Roscoff, confided to Luzel in the second half of the nineteenth century: "A tailor I knew told me that one day he was doing his rounds at a farm near Saint-Pol-de-Léon. He was alone in the house, and as he lifted his hands to eye level to thread his needle, he spied an imp sitting on a rafter and mimicking his movements. He remained motionless for a moment, seized with astonishment; then he dropped his needle, thread and scissors and fled. He had no need to be scared, for imps will do you no harm unless you harm them first."[154]

IMPS ON HORSEBACK

While familiar imps usually live on farms and in houses, they spend the greater part of their time in the stables, where they take care of the horses. They carefully groom, rub down, currycomb and brush their charges, and even plait their manes. Guillaume d'Auvergne, archbishop of Paris early in the thirteenth century, reported that "in the stables there are wax lamps which

154. François-Marie Luzel, *Nouvelles veillées bretonnes,* 1856–1894, reprint, PUR/Terre de Brume, 1997.
155. Guillaume d'Auvergne, *De Universo,* tome II, Paris, 1674.

seem to let droplets of wax fall onto the manes and necks of the horses; their manes are intricately plaited."[155]
Another witness reported how a groom engaged an imp "who,

for the past six years, had spent his time winding the clock and currycombing the horses. He carried out both these tasks with such exactitude that, one morning, I was curious to see how he did it: I was astonished to see the currycomb fly over the horse's rump, without any visible sign of a hand guiding it…"[156] Le Calvez explains that "their preferred lodgings are the stables and the hayloft above. During the night, from the hayloft and through the open bay over the rack, the imp throws armfuls of the best and sweetest hay to his favourite horses. If the wagoner is a 'potr gentil' or good man, if he loves

his horses and says no ill of the imps, he may be sure that on Saturday evenings when he goes to the barber to listen to the *raconteur* tell his tales, or on Sundays when he stays longer than necessary at the *local tavern, or with his sweetheart*, his horses will want for nothing; the hayrack will always be full, the manger full of oats, the troughs full of fresh water, and the next day he will find his horses well groomed and their manes plaited."[157]
In Finistère, they believe that the imps who care for horses are really former farm hands

who neglected their duties during their lifetime, and now are condemned to come back eternally to carry out this work. But others believe that, in most cases, the stable spirits are not ghosts, but real imps.

FIGHTING IMPS

Collin de Plancy affirms that the word "lutin" comes from the French *lutter*, meaning "to fight": "Lutins get their name from the fact that they love fighting with men. There was one from Thermesse who fought with anyone who came to that town. Furthermore, these creatures are never rough or violent in the games they play."[158] But lutin may also come from the Old French *hutin*, meaning stubborn or quarrelsome. King Louis X of France was nicknamed "le Hutin". From the same etymology, "utinet" refers to the cooper's hammer. The contraction of "le hutin"

gave "l'hutin" then "lutin". Many first-hand accounts attest to the outstanding strength of imps, which far exceeds their tiny size. According to a thirteenth-century German fable: "A Norwegian accompanied by a bear stopped for the night at a peasant's house, but the house was haunted by an imp of the following description: he measured three spans, was extraordinarily strong, wore a red cap, and was in the habit of turning furniture and utensils upside down. In the middle of the night he came out of his hiding place and came closer to the fire to warm himself; when he saw the bear sleeping by the hearth, he struck it, and a rude battle ensued. The next morning the imp told the peasant that he was leaving, and would not return as long as the big cat (the bear) remained in the house."[159]

LUTINS, LUTINEURS AND IMPISH IMPS

"Lutin" also gave the French verb "lutiner", meaning "to tease, or torment like a lutin".[160] Some of these spirits "lutinent" girls' hair: while they are sleeping they tangle and knot the hair into what is known as a "lutin's ladder".

The horse is the imp's most treasured possession

156. Gabrielle de Paban, *Histoire des fantômes et des démons qui se sont montrés parmi les hommes*, Paris, 1819.

157. G. Le Calvez, *Les Lutins dans le pays de Tréguer*, "Revue des traditions populaires", 1886.

158. Collin de Plancy, *Dictionnaire infernal*, 1825–1826.

159. *Der Schretel und Der Wazzerbär*, "Le Lutin et l'Ours", cited by Pierre Dubois, *La Grande Encyclopédie des lutins*, Hoëbeke, 1992.

160. Larousse du XXe siècle.

They also have the annoying habit of hiding everyday objects in the most impossible places. So whenever keys are lost, it is always best to begin looking in the most improbable spots such as the salt cannister, the dirty linen basket or a broiling pot in the kitchen. For those are the most likely places an imp might have hidden them.

These waggish little teasers take great delight in playing tricks which are in very poor taste. An eyewitness account dating from the nineteenth century describes the plaguey behaviour of one particularly persistent imp: "While not nasty, he constantly played his impish tricks on one old woman who looked after her master's house while he was away over the winter. When the old lady dozed off in front of the fire, while winding wool onto her distaff, the imp twisted the thread into huge knots, then gleefully wakened her with loud claps of thunder, which almost scared her to death; or else, he tangled her thread, pushed her spindle into the fire, using a candle, set alight the tow she had prepared for spinning, or threw great quantities of salt into her milk broth. Other times he would take out her hairpins, leaving her hair in disarray, or he would draw her a fine black mou-stache with coal; once the little devil even had the cheek to hang an iron trivet around her neck, laughing all the while."[161] But this kind of impish behaviour eventually wears thin, to the point where the victims consider them to be nothing less than demons. Collin de Plancy describes it thus: "Imps are demons who are more mischievous than wicked. They take pleasure in tormenting people, and are happy to frighten rather than really hurt them. Cardan tells of a friend who slept in a room which was haunted by imps. One night he felt a cold, limp hand like a wet rag pass across his face and neck, and try to force his mouth open. He was very careful not to yawn, but waking with a start, he heard great guffaws of laughter, yet could see nothing in the room."[162] The author goes on to describe how, after carrying out their high-jinks every night, these merry fellows would gather in cellars to "guzzle good wines".

ROGUE IMPS

The *Robert French Dictionary* shows the verb "imper", as meaning firstly "to tease", but also "to harass a woman by taking small liberties for fun", as we find in the well-known proverb:
Around wine and young girls
Is where the imp twirls.
There are imps who frequent loose girls, especially in Italy, where libertine imps such as the *barabao*, a baudy imp from Venice, change into cotton threads so as to slip unseen into the bodices of young ladies, and then proceed to yell at the top of their voices: "Ah, what fun touching titties!", or else hide at the bottom of bidets so as to more closely inspect ladies' *derrières*. The *massariol* is a lewd and lascivious imp from northern Italy, "a little farmhand" who hires himself

Illustration:
© Sandrine Gestin

161. Alfred Fouquet,
Légendes, contes et
chansons populaires du
Morbihan, Cauderan,
Vannes, 1857.
162. Collin de Plancy,
Dictionnaire infernal,
1825–1826.

out in summer for the harvest and hay-making season; but at night he is transformed into panties, a brassiere or a washcloth, the better to caress sleeping farm girls and even kiss their nipples, for that is the only wage he asks for.[163] Then in Tuscany there is the *linchetto*, a nasty imp who inspires erotic dreams in women and makes men impotent. To prevent this devilish killjoy from working his evil, the Tuscan beauties have a method: when they invite their beloved into their bed, and before any lovemaking, they take care to pluck one of their long, curly pubic hairs, which they give to the *linchetto*, with instructions to straighten it before morning. While the imp wrestles with this impossible task, the lovers are free to pursue their sensual pleasures to their heart's content.[164]

Imps according to Anatole Le Braz

In his correspondance with the folklore specialist Evans Wentz, Anatole Le Braz, author of the *La Légende de la Mort* (The Legend of Death), describes his childhood memories in Brittany, where he was rocked in his cradle by household imps:

"Formerly every house had its own. It was something like the little Roman household god Penat. Now visible, now invisible, it presided over all the acts of domestic life. Nay more; it shared in them, and in the most effective manner. Inside the house it helped the servants, blew up the fire on the hearth, supervised the cooking of the food for men or beasts, quieted the crying of the babe lying in the bottom of the cupboard, and prevented worms from settling in the pieces of bacon hanging from the beams. Similarly there fell within its sphere the management of the byres and stables: thanks to it the cows gave milk abounding in butter, and the horses had round croups and shining coats. It was, in a word, the good genius of the house, but conditionally on every one paying to it the respect to which it had the right. If neglected, ever so little, its kindness changed into spite, and there was no unkind trick of which it was not capable towards people who had offended it, such as upsetting the contents of the pots on the hearth, entangling wool round distaffs, making tobacco unsmokeable, mixing a horse's mane in inextricable confusion, drying up the udders of cows, or stripping the backs of sheep. Therefore care was taken not to annoy it. Careful attention was paid to all its habits and humours. Thus, in my parents' house, our old maid Filie never lifted the trivet from the fire without taking the precaution of sprinkling it with water to cool it, before putting it away at the corner of the hearth. If you asked her the reason for this ceremony, she would reply to you: 'To prevent the lutin burning himself there, if, presently, he sat on it.'"

163 and 164. Nancy Arrowsmith and George Moorse, *A Field Guide to the Little People*, Pocket Books, New York, 1977.

*Nis, nils,
niägruisar,
tomtus*

Nisses, tomtes

Nis, nils, niägruisar (Faroe Isles), tomtus

Nisses, sometimes called *nisse good-dreng,* or "good-boy nisses", are helpful imps to be found in Denmark, Norway, Finland, on the Baltic coast and in the Faroe Isles. Clothed in green and wearing red caps, they assume the form of jovial little old fellows, with faces like shrivelled apples trimmed with a white beard.

They live on farms, and help with work in the fields as well as household chores. They are very faithful, as are the brownies of Scotland, but they cannot stand noise or quarrelling. On the other hand, they adore music, and play the violin brilliantly. On winter nights they skate for hours on the frozen lakes.

On Christmas Eve it is they, and not Father Christmas, who bring the children presents, to the point where some think that Father Christmas is nothing more than a nisse who has grown considerably, both upwards and outwards. On that special night it is customary to leave something for them near the fireplace: a small glass of milk, a few cake crumbs, or a pinch of tobacco. It is also nisses who, at the winter solstice when nights and days are equal, go and search for the sunshine, which they bring back symbolically in the form of a holly branch.

The kirkegrim of Norway are nisses who live in churches, rather than on farms.

NILS HOLGERSSON'S
TOMTE

Tomtes of tomtgubbe, "the old man of the house", are familiar imps in Sweden, and rather similar to the Norwegian and Danish nisses. They also live on farms, and are placid by nature.

Tomtes are particularly good with children, and act as their

playmates, their guides and their conscience. It was a tomte who accompanied Nils Holgersson in his travels around Sweden, in the novel by Selma Lagerlöf: "Of course, the boy had heard of tomtes, but never imagined that they could be so tiny. The one who was sitting on the edge of the trunk was no bigger than the palm of your hand. His face was old and wrinkled, but he had no whiskers; he was dressed in a long black cloak, short trousers and a wide-brimmed black hat. He looked very spick and span, with lace at his neck and wrists, buckled shoes, and garters twisted into rosettes."[165]

Servants

Servans, sarvans, chervans, folatons, foulta, napfhans, the pâtre, Jeannot, Jean of the Bolieta

Servants are domesticated mountain imps which are found mainly in the Valais region of Switzerland, in the Alps, in Northern Italy and in the Pyrenees Basque country. They assume the form of jovial little fellows entirely dressed in red.

Their main task is to tend the cows. These good little shepherds lead them up into the moutains, where the grass is sweet and tender, singing as they go:

"*Pommette, Balette! Pass where I pass, and from the rocks you'll not fall.*"

For Alfred Maury, the servants of Perche "take care of the animals, and sometimes run the currycomb over the horses with an invisible hand. In Vendée, where they are not so agreeable, they often amuse themselves by pulling the horses' manes. Generally these curious creatures are happy with little enough, but they do expect something for their efforts."[166]

To ensure that they remain in their good books, and to repay them for their services, the peasants in the canton of Vaud

Servans, sarvans, chervans, folatons, foulta, Napfhans, le pâtre, Jeannot, Jean de la Bolieta

165. Selma Lagerlöf, *Le Merveilleux Voyage de Nils Holgersson à travers la Suède*, translated by M. de Gouvernain and L. Grumbach, Actes Sud, 1990.
166. Alfred Maury, *Les Fées au Moyen Âge*, Paris, 1843.

Illustration:
© Sandrine Gestin

Swiss servants are devoted cowherds

offer their servants the best of the morning cream; otherwise the servants get up to innumerable pranks at the expense of humans, such as curdling the milk, replacing freshly milled flour with sand or dead leaves, or tying the cows' tails together. They are also fond of tangling skeins of wool which the women leave on their spindles, as related by Huges of Mons, in 1723: "Around a footstool beside the hearth he twisted the threads which Amica, Nicolas's wife, had taken great pains to prepare for weaving into cloth; they were so tangled and knotted that it was impossible to undo them. In the light of day, several people clearly saw them and, astonished that someone would do such a thing, declared that such convoluted knotwork could not have been done by humans."[167]

167. Cited by Claude Lecouteux, *Les Nains et les Elfes au Moyen Âge*, Imago, 1988.

HOW TO GET RID OF THEM

When these servants become too troublesome, you will surely see the back of them by hanging a knife on the stable wall, or hanging a stone with a hole through the middle from the ceiling. Or else by tipping a sackful of millet on the ground,

because, according to a strange Fairyland law, they would then be obliged to count it all, grain by grain.

FERDINAND AND ARIEL.
SIR J.E.MILLAIS, BART. P.R.A.

Here ends Volume I of
The Encyclopedia of Fantasy.

The theme of Volume II will be

Fantastic beasts

including dragons, unicorns, phoenix, griffons, serres, cockatrices, basilisks, hydra, salamanders, marine serpents, malebestes, phenomenal beasts and other creatures from the supernatural and from ancient cryptozoological writings; their fabulous origins, their appearance, their symbolic significance, their virtues and their vices; how to observe and tame them, or ward them off.

Index: People of the light

Bibliography

Les Admirables Secrets d'Albert le Grand, suivi de *Secrets merveilleux de la magie naturelle et cabalistique du Petit Albert,* reprint, Nouvel Office d'Édition, 1965.

ARRAS, Jean d'. *Le Roman de Mélusine,* 1387.

ARROWSMITH, Nancy and George MOORSE. *A Field Guide to the Little People,* Pocket Books, New York, 1977.

AUVERGNE, Guillaume d'. *De Universo,* tome II, Paris, 1674.

BARANDIARAN, José Miguel de. *Mythologie basque,* Annales Pyrénéennes.

BARKER, Cicely Mary. *Le Jardin féerique,* traduit par Béatrice Vierne, présenté par Pierre Dubois, Hoëbeke, 2004.

BELLAMY, Félix. *La Forêt de Bréchéliant,* Rennes, 1896.

BERBIGUIER. *Le Fléau des farfadets, ou tous les démons ne sont pas de l'autre monde,* 1821.

BERNARD, Véronique and Sylvie DELASSUS. *Fées et princes charmants,* Nil Éditions, 1996.

BESANCON, Dominique. *Fées, naïades et nymphes,* Terre de Brume, 2000.

Bestiaires du Moyen Âge, traduits et présentés par Gabriel Bianciotto, Stock/Moyen Âge, 1980.

BOURA, Olivier. *Les Atlantides, généalogie d'un mythe,* Arléa, 1993.

BRASEY, Édouard. *Démons et merveilles,* Le Chêne, 2002.

BRASEY, Édouard. *Enquête sur l'existence des fées et des esprits de la nature,* J'ai Lu, « Aventure secrète » no 4753, 1998.

BRASEY, Édouard. *Fées et elfes,* Pygmalion, 1999.

BRASEY, Édouard. *Géants et dragons,* Pygmalion, 2000.

BRASEY, Édouard. *Nains et gnomes,* Pygmalion, 1999.

BRASEY, Édouard. *Sirènes et ondines,* Pygmalion, 1999.

BRASEY, Édouard. *Sorcières et démons,* Pygmalion, 2000.

BRASEY, Édouard. *Le Guide du chasseur de fées,* Le Pré aux Clercs, 2005.

BRIGGS, Katharine. *A Dictionary of Fairies,* Penguin Books, London, 1976.

BULTEAU, Michel. *Mythologie des filles des eaux,* Éditions du Rocher, 1982.

CAMBRY, Jacques. *Voyage dans le Finistère,* 1799, reprint, Brest, 1836.

CERESOLE. *Légendes des Alpes vaudoises,* Lausanne, 1885.

CERQUAND. J.-F., *Études de mythologie grecque : Les Sirènes,* Didier et Cie, 1873.

La Chanson des Niebelungen, traduit de l'allemand par Maurice Colleville et Ernest Tonnelat, Aubier, 1944, ou traduit du moyen-haut-allemand par Danielle Buschinger et Jean-Marc Pastré, « L'Aube des peuples », Gallimard, 2001.

CHAUSSE, Sylvie. Christophe Durual et Philippe-Henri Turin, *Les Ogres,* Albin Michel, 1993.

CHESNEL, A. de. *Dictionnaire des superstitions, erreurs, préjugés et traditions populaires où sont exposées les croyances superstitieuses des temps anciens et modernes,* tome XX de l'Encyclopédie théologique, 1856.

CURRAN, Bob. *A Field Guide to Irish Fairies,* and *Guide pratique des esprits irlandais,* Appletree Press, 1997.

DELAPORTE, P. V. *Du merveilleux dans la littérature sous le règne de Louis XIV,* Paris, 1891.

DELMAS, Marie-Charlotte. *Superstitions et croyances des pays de France,* Le Chêne, 2003.

DELMAS, Marie-Charlotte. *Sur la trace des fées,* Glénat, 2004.

DONTENVILLE, Henri. *La France mythologique,* Henri Veurier, 1988.

DOPPAGNE, Albert. *Esprits et génies du terroir,* Duculot, 1977.

DUBOIS, Pierre. *La Grande encyclopédie des lutins,* Hoëbeke, 1992.

DUBOIS, Pierre. *La Grande encyclopédie des fées,* Hoëbeke, 1996.

DUBOIS, Pierre. *La Grande encyclopédie des elfes,* Hoëbeke, 2003.

DURVILLE, Henri. *Les Fées,* Perthuis, 1950.

ERASMUS. *Des prodiges.*

FAUST, Dr. Johannes. *Magia Naturalis et Innaturalis, oder Dreifacher Höllenzwang,* Passau, 1505.

FOIX, V. *Sorcières et loups-garous dans les Landes,* Auch, 1904.

FOUQUET, Alfred. *Légendes, contes et chansons populaires du Morbihan,* Cauderan, Vannes, 1857.

FOURNIVAL, Richard de. *Bestiaire d'amour*, mis en français moderne par Gabriel Bianciotto, Stock/Moyen Âge, 1980.

FRANCE, Anatole. *At the Sign of the Queen Pedauque*, and *La Rôtisserie de La Reine Pédauque*, Paris, 1893.

FRANCE, Marie de. *Lais*, traduits par Alexandre Micha, Flammarion, 1994.

FROUD, Brian and Allan LEE. *Les Fées*, Albin Michel, 1979.

GALLAIS, Pierre. *La Fée à la fontaine et à l'arbre*, Éditions Rodopi, Amsterdam, 1992.

GARINET, Jules. *La Sorcellerie en France: histoire de la magie jusqu'au XIXe siècle*, Paris, 1818, reprint, François Beauval, 1970.

GLOT, Claudine and Michel LE BRIS. *Fées, elfes, dragons et autres créatures des royaumes de féerie*, Abbaye de Daoulas, Hoëbeke, 2003.

GRAVES, Robert. *Les Mythes grecs*, traduit de l'anglais par Mounir Hafez, Fayard, 1967.

GUAITA, Stanislas de. *Le Temple de Satan*, 1915.

GRICE, F. *Folk-Tales of the North Country*, Nelson, London & Edinburgh, 1944.

GRIMM, Jacob. *Teutonic Mythology*, 1880–1888.

GRIMM, Jacob and Wilhelm. *Les Contes*, deux volumes, traduits de l'allemand par Armel Guerne, Flammarion, 1967.

GRUN, Karl. *Les Esprits élémentaires*, Verviers, 1891.

GUGENHEIM-WOLFF, Anne. *Le Monde extraordinaire des fées*, Éditions de Vecchi, 2002.

HEDELIN, François. *Des satyres, brutes, monstres et démons*, Paris, 1627.

HENDERSON, William. *Folk-Lore of the Northern Counties*, Folk-Lore Society, London, 1879.

HERODOTUS. *Histories*.

HESIODUS. *Theogony*.

HOMER. *L'Odyssée*, traduit par Victor Bérard, Gallimard, La Pléiade, 1955.

HUYGEN, Will and Rien POORTVLIET. *Les Gnomes*, Albin Michel, 1979.

JEZEQUEL, Patrick and Bénédicte MORANT. *Halloween – Sorcières, lutins, fantômes et autres croquemitaines*, Avis de Tempête, 1997.

JOHNSON, Walter. *Folk-Memory*, 1908.

KEIGHTLEY, Thomas. *The World Guide to Gnomes, Fairies, Elves and Other Little People*, Avenel Books, New York, 1978.

KIPLING, Rudyard. *Puck of Pook's Hill*, 1906.

KIPLING, Rudyard. *Rewards and Fairies*, 1910.

KIRK, Robert. *The Secret Commonwealth*, 1691 and *La République mystérieuse*, Éditions Rémy Salvator, 1896.

LE MEN, René-François. *Traditions et Superstitions de la Basse-Bretagne*, « Revue celtique », 1870–1872.

LA FONTAINE, Jean de. *Fables*, 1668–1678.

LA MOTTE-FOUQUE, Frédéric de. *Ondine*, 1811.

LAGERLOF, Selma. *The Wonderful Adventures of Nils Holgersson*, and *Le Merveilleux voyage de Nils Holgersson à travers la Suède*, traduction de M. de Gouvernain et L. Grumbach, Acte Sud, 1990.

LATINI, Brunetto. *Livre du trésor*, mis en français moderne par Gabriel Bianciotto, Stock/Moyen Âge, 1980.

LE CALVEZ, G. *Les Lutins dans le pays de Tréguer*, « Revue des traditions populaires », 1886.

LE STUM, Philippe. *Fées, korrigans et autres créatures fantastiques de Bretagne*, Editions Ouest-France, 2001.

LE ROUGE, Gustave. *La Mandragore magique*, 1912.

LECOUTEUX, Claude. *Mélusine et le chevalier au cygne*, Imago, 1997.

LECOUTEUX, Claude. *Les Nains et les elfes au Moyen Âge*, Imago 1988.

LECOUTEUX, Claude. *Petit dictionnaire de mythologie allemande*, Éditions Entente, 1991.

LUZEL, François-Marie. *Notes de voyage*, 1873, reprint, Terre de Brume, 1997.

LUZEL, François-Marie. *Nouvelles veillées bretonnes*, 1856–1894, reprint, PUR/Terre de Brume, 1997.

MACHEN, Arthur. *Le Petit peuple*, 1927, various writings translated from English by Norbert Gaulard in *Chroniques du petit peuple*, Terre de Brume, 1998.

MAC MANUS, Dermot. *The Middle Kingdom – The Faerie World of Ireland*, Max Parrish and Co Ltd., 1959.

MAC RITCHIE, David. *The Testimony of Tradition*, Kegan Paul, London, 1890.

MAP, Walter, *De Nugis Curialium*, London, 1924.

MARKALE, Jean. *La Grande épopée des Celtes*, cinq volumes, Pygmalion, 1997.

MARKALE, Jean. *Petit dictionnaire de mythologie celtique*, Éditions Entente, 1986.

MARLIAVE, Olivier. de, *Petit dictionnaire de mythologies basque et pyrénéenne*, Éditions Entente.

MARLIAVE, Olivier de. *Trésor de la mythologie pyrénéenne*,

Annales Pyrénéennes.

MAURY, Alfred. *Les Fées au Moyen Âge,* Paris, 1843.

MERINDOL, Ismaël. *Traité de faërie,* 1466, Bibliothèque nationale de Prague.

MERRIEN, Jean. *Le Légendaire de la mer,* Robert Laffont, 1968, reprint, Terre de Brume, 1994.

MESLIN, Michel. *Le Merveilleux – L'Imaginaire et les croyances en Occident,* Bordas, 1984.

MIGNOT, Dr Roger. *Les Fées franc-comtoises,* chez l'auteur, 1984.

Les Mille et Une Nuits, traduction de Bencheikh et Miquel, Folio, Gallimard.

MONTFAUCON DE VILLARS, Abbé. *Le Comte de Gabalis,* Paris, *1670.*

MONTS, Karl des. *Légendes des Pyrénées,* Paris, sd.

MORVAN, Françoise. *Vie et mœurs des lutins bretons,* Babel, 1998.

MOZZANI, Éloïse. *Magie et superstitions de la fin de l'Ancien Régime à la Restauration,* Robert Laffont, 1988.

NERVAL, Gérard de. *Lorely, Souvenirs d'Allemagne,* 1852.

NICAISE, Claude. *Discours sur les sirènes,* Paris, 1691.

OVID. *Métamorphoses,* trad. G. T. Villenave.

PABAN, Gabrielle de. *Histoire des fantômes et des démons qui se sont montrés parmi les hommes,* Paris, 1819.

PAGE, Michael and Robert INGPEN. *Encyclopedia of Things That Never Were,* Dragon's World Ltd, 1985.

PARACELSUS. *A Book on Nymphs, Sylphs, Pygmies and Salamanders and on the Other Spirits,* and *Traité des nymphes, sylphes, pygmées, salamandres et autres êtres,* 1566, traduit par Sylvie Paris, C. Lacour Éditeur, Nîmes, 1998.

PERNETY, Dom Antoine-Joseph. *Dictionnaire mytho-hermétique, dans lequel on trouve les allégories fabuleuses des poètes, les métaphores, les énigmes et les termes barbares des philosophes hermétiques expliqués,* Paris, Delalain aîné, 1787.

PHILLPOTTS, Beatrice. *Le Livre des fées – Voyage au pays de Faerie,* Hors Collection, 2000.

PHILLPOTTS, Beatrice. *Mermaids,* New York, Ballantine Books, 1980.

PICARD, Charles. « Néréides et Sirènes : observations sur le folklore hellénique de la mer », in *Annales de l'École des Hautes Études de Gand,* 1938.

PLANCY, Collin de. *Dictionnaire infernal,* 1825–1826.

PLATO. *Critias.*

PLINY THE ELDER. *Historia naturalis.*

QUELLIEN, N. *Contes et nouvelles du pays de Tréguier,* Paris, 1899.

Revue des traditions populaires, 1886.

ROSE, Carol. *Spirits, Fairies, Gnomes and Goblins – An Encyclopedia of the Little People,* ABC-CLIO Inc, 1996.

ROSSETTI, Christina. *Goblin Market,* and *Le Marché des gobelins,* 1862.

RUAUD, André-François. *Le Dictionnaire féerique,* Éditions de l'Oxymore, 2002.

SAND, George. *Légendes rustiques,* 1858.

SCOT, Reginald. *The Discovery of Witchcraft,* London, 1584.

SCOTT, Michael. *Irish Folk & Fairy Tales,* Warner Books, 1989.

SCOTT, Sir Walter. *Letters on Demonology and Witchcraft,* London, 1830 and *Histoire de la démonologie et de la sorcellerie,* traduction de M. Defauconpret, Furne Éditeur, Paris, 1832.

SHAKESPEARE, William. *The Tempest and A Mid-Summer Nights' Dream.*

SCHWOB, Marcel. « Les Stryges », *Cœur double,* 1891.

SEBILLOT, Paul. Croyances, *Mythes et légendes des pays de France* (1904–1906), Omnibus, 2002.

SEIGNOLLE, Claude. *Contes, récits et légendes des pays de France,* quatre volumes, Omnibus, 1997.

SEMUR, Gratien de. *Traité des erreurs et des préjugés,* Paris, A. Levasseur, 1843.

SIKES, Wirt. *British Goblins,* London, Sampson Low, Marston, Searle and Rivington, 1880,

SOUVESTRE, Émile. *Le Foyer breton,* Paris, 1852.

STURLUSON, Snorri. *L'Edda, récits de mythologie nordique,* traduit du vieil-islandais par François-Xavier Dillmann, « L'Aube des peuples », Gallimard, 1991.

TOLKIEN, J.R.R. *Lord of the Rings,* and *Le Seigneur des Anneaux,* Christian Bourgois, 1972.

TOLKIEN, J.R.R. *Faërie, various writings translated from English,* Christian Bourgois, 1974.

TRANOIS, Corentin. *Coricanets,* « Revue de Bretagne », tome IV, Rennes, 1834.

VERUSMOR. *Voyage en Basse-Bretagne,* Jollivet, Guingamp, 1855.

WENZ, W. Y. Evans. *The Fairy-Faith in Celtic Countries,* London, H. Frowde, 1911.

WILDE, F. S. *Ancient Legends of Ireland,* London, 1887.